God bless you.

Robert L. Wallace

2020

The Ssese Principles

By

Robert L. Wallace

Bloomington, IN Milton Keynes, UK

authorHOUSE

AuthorHouse™
1663 Liberty Drive, Suite 200
Bloomington, IN 47403
www.authorhouse.com
Phone: 1-800-839-8640

AuthorHouse™ UK Ltd.
500 Avebury Boulevard
Central Milton Keynes, MK9 2BE
www.authorhouse.co.uk
Phone: 08001974150

This book is a work of non-fiction. Unless otherwise noted, the author
and the publisher make no explicit guarantees as to the accuracy of
the information contained in this book and in some cases, names of
people and places have been altered to protect their privacy.

First published by AuthorHouse 2/23/2006

ISBN: 1-4208-0343-3 (e)
ISBN: 1-4208-0341-7 (sc)
ISBN: 1-4208-0342-5 (dj)

Library of Congress Control Number: 2004097807

Printed in the United States of America
Bloomington, Indiana

This book is printed on acid-free paper.

Table of Contents

Preface

Dear Believers,

If you are like me and the most important thing in your life is to bring pleasure and honor to God, then this is the book for you. Jesus' message of peace, love, patience, forgiveness, of feeding the hungry, providing shelter to the homeless, and instilling hope into the hopeless holds universal appeal – even to those among us who have not yet embraced His leadership in their lives.

During my multiple efforts of working with entrepreneurs, businesses, government officials, and the spiritual community, God began revealing to me the contents of this book in multiple dreams and admonitions. In these dreams, He has shown me that embedded within the Bible's theological foundations are kernels of business and wealth creation wisdom that will provide encouragement and direction to individuals looking to use their God-given assets to provide for the physical needs of their family and concurrently expand and fortify the Kingdom of God during their time on a planet with numbered days.

I pray that you will read these principles with an open mind and a humble heart and earnestly be about the business of using the wealth and assets that God has entrusted to you to accelerate the day when Jesus and the hosts of heaven will come hurtling through the dim mist of eternity and take us home.

I pray that we will all be ready!
Robert L. Wallace

Dedication

This book is dedicated to the Lamb of God (Jesus Christ) who left the Holy confines of heaven, wrapped his divinity in the sinful flesh of humanity, and sacrificed Himself on the cross for my sins. He conquered the death that I deserved so that I would enjoy the eternal blessings and everlasting life that He deserves.

Ever since I decided to join the Kingdom of God and not the kingdom of Satan, God has provided me all of the help and resources that I need to fight a good fight, to keep the faith, and finish my course. First, he gave me great parents –Irene, Danny, Leon, Hezekiah, and Edith. Then He blessed me with my lovely bride of twenty-eight years – Carolyn. Not only is she my adorable bride but she is the best friend that I have in the entire world. Carolyn makes it possible for me to run the multitude of businesses and projects of which I am engaged. Together, God has blessed us with wonderful children – Bobby, Joshua, Collin, Jordan, Taylor, Ashana, Ayla, Ryan, and James.

This book is also dedicated to my big brothers –Richard, Ronald, and Randy – and my little brother –Raymond. My brothers mentored and protected me through some of the most difficult times that one could imagine. Through it all we held on to our faith, weathered the storms of life, and refused to neglect our salvation.

A special thanks to Dr. Samuel L. DeShay and the late Dr. Samson Kisekka, two great men of God who dedicated their lives to improving the condition of God's children, who reside on the continent of Africa. I am also grateful to Ms. Joyce Harris and Ms. Jeanne Youcum (Tuscarora Communications) for their editorial assistance.

I am a blessed man, not because of my material blessings but because of the people who love me and because of the One who has secured my eternal destiny through His blood.

A portion of the proceeds from this book will be used to fund the building of a clinic in the Ssese Islands, Christian education, and inner-city ministries.

Introduction

In Greek mythology, Sisyphus, a great warrior, had been condemned by the gods to push a rock to the top of a mountain, where it would of its own weight fall to the bottom. Sisyphus would shove it back up, only to have it roll down, again and again, the process continuing forever. What a torturous existence! The idea was that no punishment worse than this futile, hopeless effort.

Unfortunately, many of us today endure a Sisyphus-like existence when it comes to managing our money and accumulating wealth. Some of us go through life struggling daily to better manage our money and build wealth, making valiant efforts worthy of a noble warrior only to find that our efforts have produced insignificant results and limited options. Like Sisyphus, we try again but often find ourselves in a sad and discouraging cycle.

In an effort to break the dreaded, but very real Wealth Sisyphus Cycle, while earning my Masters of Business Administration from the Amos Tuck School of Business at Dartmouth College, I initiated a ground-breaking study to analyze the success factors and success blueprint for the new economy entrepreneurs. This study, which initially spanned more than a decade but which now is an on-going research project that already spans more than two decades and consumes my time on a daily basis, was so revolutionary that it helped change the way America looks at entrepreneurship and wealth management.

This initial research project has spawned multiple books, training tapes, workshops, seminars, our Centers for Wealth Creation through Entrepreneurship and our e-learning company, EntreTeach Learning Systems, LLC. I have had the opportunity to work with government, foreign nations, major corporations, small business institutions, and some of the most successful entrepreneurs in America. Suffice it to say, I have learned a lot from friends and partners in my journey to add intellectual value to the art of entrepreneurship.

One of the revealing lessons I have learned from this research is the relationship between entrepreneurship, wealth, and the idea of doing well by doing good. To me, this means creating wealth through entrepreneurship in such a way, that not only do you personally benefit, but others do as well, while leveraging the principles that God has provided us as enablers. The wide spread confusion around the topic of wealth creation and wealth management has caused great confusion and has resulted in people making terrible mistakes that have often led to financial ruin and disaster. As I traveled the world lecturing on entrepreneurship and its relationship to wealth creation, I made a commitment to someday write another book on how to create and manage wealth from a Godly perspective. This book is my attempt to keep that promise.

No place was more confused about the issue of wealth creation and management than the people who lived in my old childhood neighborhood. As a child growing up in the rough and tough neighborhood of the Cherry Hill community in Baltimore, Maryland, the church was often our compass as we navigated the treacherous seas of life. Although we were poor like most families in our neighborhood, our parents made sure that we were in Church multiple times a week. While I would certainly concede that the church has been a rock of hope and salvation for a dying world, many of our well-meaning spiritual leaders have mistakenly used the word of God as an impediment to wealth creation instead of as an enabler.

For example, in my church back in the old neighborhood, we were taught that money, power, business, and wealth were inherently bad and evil. If you desired any of these tenets of capitalism, you were doomed to suffer hell's fire when Jesus returned to claim His children and rid the world of the damning effects of a world lost in sin.

As a young man who spent most of his waking hours concocting new ways to make money, obtain power, and enjoy some level of business success, as well as the inherent wealth that comes with all these achievements, I was perplexed as to what was the proper synergism between my spiritual convictions and my strong desire to achieve wealth and business success. So my search began. As I prayed and began to study the Holy Scriptures for answers to my nagging questions, God began revealing to me nuggets of wisdom, through His word, about how to "build wealth from the inside out." In other words, how to do well and do good, at the same time by putting to use God's powerful and ageless principles.

What I found to my amazement from my study of the Word of God is that, contrary to what I was taught as a young child, God is not against wealth or riches. He is not against business success and the enjoyment of material possessions. What He does caution us about is not to make riches, material gain, and wealth our Gods. He admonishes us not to put anything before Him, His Kingdom, and His agenda. God reminds us that putting anything (i.e. money, wealth, possessions, sex, spouse, land, etc.) before or above God is simply idolatry and God will not allow idols to take His rightful place in our lives. In fact, all that we have, own, say or think is owned by God and is simply loaned to us while we live and should be committed to and invested in His Kingdom. The Lord can count on righteous men and women of means to carry out His Kingdom agenda and to work to accelerate the day of Jesus' second (and next to last) return.

Not only did I learn that God is not against us enjoying wealth but that He gives us the roadmap on how to achieve it! Deposited among the Holy Scriptures like nuggets of gold found in the gold mines of Johannesburg, South Africa, were the jewels of wisdom that pertain to wealth creation, wealth capturing, wealth management, and wealth maintenance. While I have read most of today's popular books on business success, wealth management, and personal success, the Holy Word of God provided me more guidance and direction on building wealth than all of these books combined.The wisdom inherent in God's word helped me to appreciate my recent visit to Africa. As a matter of fact, the idea for this book became cemented in my mind during this particular African visit to a place in the eastern region of the African continent, bordering the lands of Kenya, Tanzania, and Uganda. Our destination point, the beautiful Lake Victoria, is the world's second largest fresh water lake. Lake Victoria boasts an area of more than two hundred square miles. Nestled in the northwestern end of the lake, are the verdant Ssese Islands, eighty-four in number, pristine and serene in loveliness. Because of the near 4,000 ft. elevation of these islands, the climate is ideal year round. Of all my worldly travels, these islands are arguably one of the most beautiful destinations my wife and I have ever visited. Like the thousand islands of Canada, some of the islands are so small that it would be almost impossible to build anything of substance on them. But there are some islands in the Ssese chain that are quite large and hold great potential for commercial, residential, and retail development.

One of the larger islands is Bugala Island. This island is as large as the State of Rhode Island in the United States. Several other islands are sizeable and nearly uninhabited. In 1904, the British moved the inhabitants to the mainland for health reasons. The majority of the islanders never returned to the peaceful paradise, but chose to take up residence on the mainland. Those who did return to this beautiful, white sand, tropical island home, squeeze out a meager existence from either fishing on the lake or farming on small plots of land. This particular island is also the largest of all the islands. Now, the President of the Republic of Uganda, President Yoweri Museveni, and the people of Uganda, desire to convert it into a thriving center of business, commerce, culture, and place for spiritual rebirth.

I became aware of this "Ssese Project" through my friend and mentor, Dr. Samuel L. DeShay. Dr. DeShay, was invited by the then Prime Minister of Uganda, the late Dr. Samson Kisekka and President Museveni to assist the people of Uganda in turning the dream into a reality. Dr. DeShay's background certainly qualified him to be an advisor to the President on this project. Dr. Deshay, along with many of the leaders from the Republic of Uganda, had spent the last couple of years researching and developing the concept of an "international city." It would become Africa's twenty-first century Techno polis – a new town development that will provide the Ssese Islands and Uganda with a self-sufficient economic base.

Prior to this project, Dr. DeShay, along with his wife, Bernice A. DeShay, R.N., served in Africa as missionaries for 15 years (1960 through 1975) participating in projects analogous to this development project. He has served as the Director of three different government-owned hospitals in West Africa. Additionally, he was asked by the Nigerian government to be the Senior Medical Officer at Port Harmust. He has been responsible for the building of hospitals, schools, and churches. In 1968, while serving as the Head of the Masanga Leprosy Hospital in Sierra Leone, Dr. DeShay was instrumental in working with the

US government to bring multi-national corporations, such as IBM, to fund and develop a data base that would be used in tracking the diagnosis of the disease. Through his experience, Dr. Deshay developed a genuine empathy for African culture and population values. A graduate of Loma Linda University Medical School in California, Dr. DeShay holds several master's degrees and a Doctor of Ministry degree in Ethics from Howard University Divinity School in Washington, D.C.

Along with his commitment to the field of health, Dr. DeShay remains an entrepreneur at heart. He is currently in private practice outside Washington, D.C. and was responsible for co-founding the Plus Fifteen Corporation. The Plus Fifteen Corporation offers a new and breakthrough approach to lowering blood pressure and cholesterol levels through a series of 15 steps using a natural regimen of diet, exercise, weight control, and stress reduction.

Known as men of great vision and creativity, President Museveni, Dr. DeShay, and others on the team, immediately began envisioning what they could build on these islands to make them the most popular destination point in all of East Africa for tourists. At a time when many localities are threatened by violence and fear all around, the team thought it would be fitting and desirable that a quiet place be found away from the noise, the unrest, and the turmoil for a little spiritual reflection and contemplation.

Within this framework, the Ssese Islands concept was born. Dedicated as an International Zone of Peace, with free access to all peace-loving people and dedicated to the germination of noble thoughts and deeds, this island would be set apart. Within this zone of peace, the team of advisors dream of attracting tourists from America, Europe, Asia, and South America. Their grand and exotic vision for the islands has no limits and no boundaries. Once the zone of peace is completed, current plans include building a world-class hotel and resort on the "ten island city" along with an accredited medical hospital, smaller medical clinics, and even dedicate one of the islands for religious and spiritual revival. Home sites are currently being prepared on the western side of the Bugala Island hillsides that will be sold to American citizens and the international community who desire to live and retire on the islands. Committed to the vision that God has given them, they have stepped out on faith and transformed what was initially an abstract dream into detailed architectural and engineering drawings.

By most people's standards, the vision of this impressive group of leaders is bold, big, significant, and will require a great deal of resources, and coordination, along with a heavy dose of divine intervention. So far, the full extent of the dream has been unrealized. Yet when you spend time with Dr. DeShay and others on this team, their vision to do God's work is so compelling that it becomes infectious. Instead of seeing the remote and uninhabited beaches, through his eyes you see instead a modern airport carved into the landscape of Bugala Island and shuttles to whisk you and your guest off to your luxury lakeside room at the Yoweri Museveni Hotel (built through a partnership with the Sheraton Corporation). They envision a network of ferry boats operating to whisk the visitors between the ten islands. On Sabbath, you would be able to take a boat to the Island of Spiritual Revival where President Museveni and Dr. DeShay would invite the world's most powerful men and women of God to come preach the Gospel! The vision of this impressive team of men and women goes on and on and on and has no limits.

Dr. DeShay, as is the case with most members of this team, is a strong believer in the power and might of God so he speaks and acts as if his vision already exists and his passion for achieving it drives him each day and makes his life exciting, fun, full of suspense, and just worth living. There is no question that once his dream is fulfilled, it will bring glory and honor to God and at the same time provide an economic base and foundation of wealth for the industrious people of Uganda for many decades to come.

After you are finished reading this book, the questions that I pose to you and hopefully you will challenge yourself with are: What is your "Ssese Project" for wealth creation? What is that financial or business dream that is so big, so awesome, so far away but yet so close that it keeps you awake at night, invites you to sacrifice your time and resources, and brings a pep to your step and puts a sparkle in your eye? What dream has God given you that when you achieve it, God's power and might, will once again be recognized, He will be glorified, and His Kingdom blessed? Our individual Ssese Project compels us to ask God, what we can do for Him, instead of us always asking something from Him.

Our Ssese Projects are the things that usher us in the direction of achieving great things and in the process experiencing the full potential, power, and greatness of God. God's power to help us create and manage wealth is made perfect when we are at our weakest and our Ssese Project so big, and seemingly unachievable, that we recognize that the only way we can achieve this thing is through the divine intervention and direction of God.

The power of the ten principles of wealth creation outlined in this book are so powerful that I have called them the Ssese Principles in recognition of the fact that if you follow these tenets, you will have the ability to achieve your Ssese Project. These principles will be made perfect only when you apply them in your attempt to do something great and significant in your community, your country and, yes, the entire world. Hold on to your hat because it is going to be some ride!

An Honest Discussion Regarding Wealth

As is true with most misunderstood topics, a conversation around wealth brings to light many different meanings and interpretations. Here are a few definitions of wealth that I often use in my speeches and workshops:

• "Wealth is money you make if you're not working." (Wealth is not dependent on activity during the working hours.)

• "...a good man blesses his children's children." King Solomon –Book of Proverbs (Wealth is transferable from generation to generation.)

• "Wealth is making money while you sleep." Reginald F. Lewis – (Wealth is not time dependent.)

• A derivative of a relational definition of Wealth that I have adapted from my 20 years of research of successful entrepreneurs is this:

Wealth $= G * (M * T * I) / R$

Where: G = Wisdom of God and Kingdom Focus

M = Material Resources (land, labor and capital)

T = Technological Resources

I = Intelligence/Knowledge

R = Resistance (Resistance from Satan and his cohorts)

A simpler, yet persuasive definition of wealth is the accumulation of "stuff" that you have left over after you've paid all of your bills and met all of your physical needs.

Furthering the discussion of wealth, in my third book, "Soul Food: The 52 Principles of Black Entrepreneurial Success," I began a discussion about what wealth is and what it is not. First of all, I have always viewed wealth as being three dimensional – having width, depth, and height. Having more than enough assets to meet your needs represents the width of wealth. Having the "stuff" of life (i.e. land, money, real estate, stocks, bonds, and cash) in such abundance that it can be transferred to your children and your children's children, defines the depth of wealth. Finally, the height of wealth is having the type of resources that even if you are not working and not directly involved in the daily leveraging of those assets, they will still appreciate in value. Other forms of wealth that tend to be less valued by our society (but are just as important) include our time, our talents, and our temple (the body). Without these basic but critical assets, the creation and management of wealth would be impossible.

Building wealth is important from a Godly perspective because wealth properly managed and used multiplies the diversity of options that God's people have in life. The accumulation of wealth – financial, health, social, cultural, and political – positions individuals to be able to take advantage of opportunities and produces certain outcomes. Without a doubt, wealth does matter.

True wealth is also important because it brings real and lasting joy and has no sorrow with it. It is used to not only benefit the individual but also those people that the individual touches or who exist within the person's sphere of influence. When one is truly wealthy his/her wealth is always viewed through the expanding lens of eternity and not the temporal lens of our physical existence here on earth.

According to government statistics, the average American will live somewhere between 70 to 80 years. The life span varies based upon gender, race, and, of course, lifestyle. A physical view of life in this case would expand our planning horizon from 0-80 years, maybe. However, Godly people view wealth in a spiritual sense and so their time horizon is elongated to span from "eternity past" to "eternity future." This planning horizon takes into consideration that God was around in eternity past and from there created the universe and humankind. Man's time on earth, which is at best, a thin sliver of time called "human history," has spanned some 6,000 years so far (according to the bible). But the opportunity for us is in eternity future where we have the opportunity to spend forever and ever with God in His presence. Therefore our wealth algorithm must factor in the use of our limited physical wealth on earth as an investment for our unlimited spiritual wealth that we will inherit in eternity. We invest in eternity when we use our physical wealth to strengthen and expand the Kingdom of God during our tenure on earth.

If we view wealth through the lens of eternity, we will not come to the mistaken conclusion that wealth is simply the accumulation of material "stuff." It makes no sense to accumulate the "stuff" of life and yet live miserable, unhappy, and unhealthy lives.

True wealth is not just the accumulation of material things but it is also the enjoyment of those material things because they are used to benefit humanity, and the expansion and strengthening of the Kingdom of God.

True and Meaningful Wealth Comes From God

What many people fail to realize is that all wealth comes from God, whether they accept this reality or not. God gives us the power and means to create and the opportunity to manage it for Him. But like any prudent businessperson, He requires a return on His investment – a spiritual return on investment (SROI), if you will.

"And thou say in thine heart, my power and the might of mine hand hath gotten me this wealth. But thou shalt remember the Lord thy God: for it is He that giveth thee power to get wealth, which He may establish His covenant which he sware unto thy fathers, as it is this day. And it shall be, if thou do at all forget the Lord thy God, and walk after other gods, and serve them, and worship them, I testify against you this day that ye shall surely perish." -- Deuteronomy 8: 17-19

A key learning point from this admonition from God is that He will give us what we need to create, capture, manage, and maintain wealth but in return for Him giving us this wealth creation gift, God requires that we then use this wealth to advance and expand His Kingdom on this earth. What I think is implied in this message is that the level or quantity of wealth that God delivers to humanity will be different and vary from person to person. Some will be allowed to amass large sums of wealth while others will have to make due with less, but the investment commitment of that wealth remains the same whether you are very wealthy or not so wealthy.

The message embedded in this scriptural text and which is presented in this book is the fact that God has levels of blessings that He desires to shower upon us. But our lack of understanding and implementation of these key biblical principles of wealth management slows down, reduces, and in some cases even negates our receipt of these gifts from God. One of the purposes of this book is to help you claim all of the blessings that God has reserved for your enjoyment and as resources to benefit the Kingdom.

This book is not about showing you how to get rich quick. If this is what you desire, you will find dozens of books on the market that will lead you in that direction. As a matter of fact, this book is not about getting rich at all, unless that is what God desires to give you. Instead, it is about preparing and equipping yourself with the time-tested realities and promises that God has given to us all. This book is about reaching that wonderful state with God where you are not only in receipt of what He has for you but taking the next step, which is to use those blessings to strengthen and expand the Kingdom of God on this Earth in your own personal life.

Overview of the Ssese Principles of Wealth

The ten principles are based upon the wealth building tenets that are so clearly outlined in the Holy Bible and shadowed in other religious documents. If properly followed, these principles provide proven and tested guidelines for achieving sustainable levels of material wealth while not violating one's relationship with God and remaining in a position where the wealth can be enjoyed – not only by the individual but by all people that are captured in the individual's "sphere of influence."

In studying the ten principles of wealth creation it is important for you to not allow yourself to be misled by false doctrines. I recognize two false doctrines of wealth: the principle of poverty and the principle of wealth.

The principle of poverty suggests that poverty is equivalent to godliness. It mistakenly supports the belief that the poorer you are the more spiritual you are and consequently the closer your walk with God must be. Those who subscribe to this doctrine cite examples in the Bible of how various prophets, disciples, and Jesus Christ himself, lived life without material riches, and in some cases, lived as the homeless. Those who follow this doctrine demonize success and criticize those who are successful; they use this principle as a way to comfort those who are impoverished. Followers of this doctrine try to convince others that they should not worry about accumulating wealth in this life and only concern themselves with accumulating riches in the afterlife. The only hope that they leave their constituents is the glorious hope of heaven.

Opposite to the principle of poverty is the principle of wealth. Those who follow and believe in the principle of wealth equate wealth with godliness. The wealthier you are the more blessed you are and consequently the more favored by God you must be. These individuals can also quote examples of how God materially blessed favored people in the Bible. They will cite the examples of King David, King Solomon, Job, Abraham, and others to make their point that wealth is indeed equated with godliness. Many of the Scribes and Pharisees of Jesus' day subscribed to this principle, which made it easier for them to devalue Him who was sent to save them from their sins. Believers of this doctrine have mistakenly concluded that their identity and acceptance by God is a function of how much "stuff" they own.

From my research and based upon my experience, both of these principles are flawed. As a matter of fact, in a particular workshop on "Building Wealth from the Inside Out," I steer clients away from both extremes – the principle of poverty and the principle of wealth – concluding that no honor exists in either of these two impostors. Instead, I encourage clients to focus on the ten principles (principles) that are outlined below. These ten principles are broken into three different groupings:

- Principles that are actuated by God. These principles define the things that God is doing or has promised to do for His children, and for those who serve Him. These are referred to as G-Principles.

- Principles that define the process by which we are to interface with God and receive His blessings. These are defined as P-Principles.

- Principles that define what our individual responsibilities are. These are defined as I-Principles.

The ten principles are grouped as follows:

God Promised Principles

The Principle of Leverage

The Omni-X Principle

The Principle of Ownership

The Principle of Love

The Principle of Wealth Transfer

Process Based Principles

The Principle of Giving Sequence

The Principle of Sowing and Reaping

The Principle of Blessing Expectation

Individual Based Principles

The Principle of Wealth Through Your Talents

The Principle of Contentment

Overview of the "Kingdom" Concept

Throughout this book I will often use the terms king and kingdom to explain the ten wealth building principles. To consolidate our understanding of this terminology and how it fits into the discussion, a brief overview of these terms is appropriate.

Years ago, in a distant kingdom, the first recorded war was initiated. This war would serve to define humanity on earth and set the stage for the largest and most intense drama ever to be experienced by humankind. This war or great controversy as some have come to call it was waged in heaven between God (the Creator of the universe and the author of life) and Satan (a very special angel created by God Himself). The war broke out because, like many of us, Satan wanted to displace God from His position of power and authority. God's only begotten son Michael (Jesus) and His army of loyal angels did battle with Satan and his loyal angels (approximately one-third of the angels of heaven) and for a while there was great turmoil and unrest in the holy confines of heaven.

But, as will always be the case, the forces of evil were no match for the forces of good, so Satan and his army was soundly defeated and ultimately lost their place in heaven. As initial punishment, Satan and his army were kicked out of heaven and were hurled to the Earth, where they were allowed to set up another kingdom. This kingdom would be instituted among humankind, and Satan thought that with the combination of his evil angels (who were dispelled from heaven along with him) and the portion of humanity that he could convince to join forces with him, that he could finally defeat the forces of God and rule over the Earth. Consequently, since being confined to the earth, Satan has spent all of his time and resources trying to get humankind to live in his kingdom instead of God's Kingdom.

This great controversy between the Kingdom of God and the kingdom of Satan, between good and evil, continues to this very day. Whether we know it or not, we are all players in this war. We are either on the side of good or the side of evil. We are either members of God's Kingdom or Satan's kingdom so it is important to understand and appreciate the concept of kingdoms.

Typically a kingdom is made up of four major components. Every kingdom has a king, a domain, rules of engagement, and subjects. To begin with, the king is the ruler and most dominant force in the kingdom. He sets the direction for the kingdom and everyone within that domain subjugates themselves to the king. God is king of the kingdom of good and Satan is king of the kingdom of evil.

But to be a true and powerful king, he must rule over a domain. The domain is the geographical territory that the king has legitimate control over. For example, the King of England had control over the country of England as well as all of the conquered territories that it forcibly controlled. The emperor of Japan had rule over the country of Japan and its territories. God's domain reaches the far corners of the absolute universe. All of the planets, celestial constellations, and galaxies are under His control. Conversely, Satan's domain is limited to the physical confines of the planet Earth. He has no influence on the other worlds throughout the universe. To hold the domain together and to create an environment where entities can coexist and meet the demands and requirements of the king, the king institutes rules, agreements, and guidelines for the subjects in the kingdom to follow. When these rules are followed there is harmony and productivity in the kingdom. When the rules are not followed, not only does harmony or productivity not exist in the kingdom, but some dire consequences are to be paid for noncompliance. In the kingdom of God the scriptures provide the rules and guidelines under which the kingdom is managed. Whether someone is Christian or Muslim or follows other religions, there are rules under which they must live to remain in harmony with God.

Lastly, there would be no Kingdom without subjects (people). You and I are the subjects of one of these two kingdoms. We get to choose the kingdom to which we belong. Make no mistake about it; you are either in God's Kingdom or Satan's kingdom. You cannot be in both kingdoms. Nor is there some neutral kingdom to be a part of so that you're able to hedge your bet. If you are not in God's Kingdom, you are automatically in Satan's kingdom, doing his bidding.

The awesome part about being in God's Kingdom is that you are not only working in partnership with other believers on this Earth but also with the heavenly hosts (angels) and the other subjects on the undiscovered worlds throughout the universe! What power and great company we keep when we pledge ourselves and our resources (i.e. time, talent, treasure, and temple) to the God of the universe.

Principle # 1: The Principle of Leverage

"…'How can we feed this huge crowd? All we have is five little loaves of bread and two small fish!' Jesus said, 'Let me have those little loaves and small fish.' When they brought Him the loaves and small fish, He asked the crowd to find some grass and sit down. He took the five little loaves and the two small fish, looked up to heaven and asked a blessing, giving thanks for what He had…everyone had enough to eat. When they were finished, the disciples picked up twelve basketsful of what was left." -- Mathew 14: 15-21

As an entrepreneur you often have to make major sacrifices to someday see the bright sunshine of success. I certainly was no exception to this rule and had often gone without to assure that the needs of my business and my family had been met.

But God is great and awesome and somewhere along the way He began to bless my business in such a way that it became possible for me to purchase nice things for my family and friends. The one area of my life that I had the most resistance to changing was in the type of car that I drove. Admittedly, I still am what the young folks call "old school." For ten years I drove this old

Volvo 240 station wagon (I still have the car and it has over 300,000 miles on it!). I had five children to clothe, feed, and educate and always felt that a "nice" car was a luxury that I didn't need to have and could live without. But after a few years of lobbying and consulting from my two older sons, Bobby and Joshua, I broke down and purchased a brand new Mercedes E500. Truth be told, they actually shamed me into buying it, but that's another story.

What a driving experience it has been! To go from an old Volvo station wagon to a high technology Mercedes Benz I must say has been exhilarating. The car is fun to drive and I feel good driving it. One day my son Bobby Jr. and I were driving to Philadelphia to attend a conference where I was to deliver a speech. As we were heading up Interstate 95, I was sharing with my son how much I enjoyed the car, and I was showing off some of the fancy features of this high tech machine. I really thought I knew my stuff and was convinced that I thoroughly understood all of the benefits that the car had to offer.

After patiently listening to his old man brag about his new toy, my son respectfully smiled at me and said "Dad, you are only using a fraction of the features of this car. When we stop for gas, let me drive, and I will show you how to really leverage all of the technology built into this vehicle." After gassing the car up, Bobby took over the wheel and completely opened my eyes to the full potential of that E 500. He proceeded to show me how you can drive the car like a sports car by shifting from the automatic transmission to a five-speed manual-transmission. He explained how the suspension of the car can be dynamically adjusted to either drive at high speeds or cruise along the highway like you are floating on a cushion of air. Later he indicated that the windshield wipers come on by themselves and adjust their speed based on the amount of moisture on the windshield and how the rearview mirror will dim or adjust itself to accommodate for the increase or decrease of light reflecting off the mirror. He went on and on and on as I sat there a little dumbfounded, pleasantly surprised, but I must admit, feeling a little foolish. For weeks I had been driving around in a $70,000 engineering marvel, but because of my ignorance and refusal to spend time studying the owner's manual, I was missing the full benefit and robust driving experience of this wonderfully engineered German driving machine.

Similar to my experience with my Mercedes, many of us go through life and never fully leverage the power and might of our God. He has provided a wonderful owner's manual (the Holy Bible) that we tend to breeze through and only open when we're broken down and sitting on the side of the road of life. If only we would spend time with it and really understand all of the wisdom, power, and direction that it gives us in managing every aspect of our lives – even our financial lives! By understanding God better, we have the opportunity and potential to leverage his awesome power to do great and marvelous things.

Leverage is such a powerful tool in life. We use it in business, high finance, engineering, physics, and, yes, the spiritual realm as well. Leverage allows an individual to accomplish more by creatively, efficiently, and effectively using the resources of others. One's power to accomplish and do great things in life is significantly enhanced when we learn to use the leveraging power of God in our lives. On our own, we are limited by time, space, matter, and distance. We are only given 24 hours each day, seven days per week, and 52 weeks per year. The resources we own are limited, especially our financial and material resources. Our power comes from our ability to "leverage" the power of God in the events of our life and in the dreams that we dream. If we take the little that we do have (time, talent, treasure, temple) and submit ourselves to God and his blueprint for our lives, He will then actuate His unlimited resources (time, talent, treasure, temple) to leverage our efforts and assist us in realizing accomplishments that will make the world sit up and take notice of us and the glorious Kingdom of God.

Tips for Implementing This Ssese Principle in Your Life

1. There is no such thing as a "self-made man" or a "self-made woman." These are two impostors that we need to remove from our midst. No one in the history of humankind has achieved financial success on their own.

2. Leverage forces us to recognize that we are all linked together on a global as well as a cosmic level. There is more global interdependency in our world now than ever before. For example

the tea we drink is grown by farmers in the Nandi District of Kenya. The rice we eat is grown by peasants in Southeast Asia. The gold we use in our electronic systems comes from the brave but underpaid miners in South Africa and Ghana. Our entire existence is intricately connected to our brothers and sisters around the world.

3. Leverage the resources of those around you, understanding that everything that exists belongs to God and He has given you access to it at the appointed time.

4. Wealth creation requires that we leverage not only our time but the time of other people. When we join human forces in the achievement of a specific goal, we are able to accomplish a lot more in a shorter period of time.

5. Likewise, the creation and management of wealth requires that we also leverage not only our treasures but the treasures of others. This is why building and nurturing a team of investors to support your business and investment endeavors is so critically important. By adding your wealth with that of others, you put yourself in a position to do bigger and potentially more lucrative deals.

6. Wealth creation also requires that we leverage the talents of others. No one person has all of the skills, knowledge, and education necessary to complete all of the tasks required for successful wealth creation and entrepreneurial success.

7. Get moving and do something!

8. Allow God to direct all of your efforts.

9. Be about the Lord's business with passion, vigor, and attitude.

A Prayer for the Wealthy Minded

El-Shaddai:

You are so great and we are so weak and insignificant. You are so wise and yet we are so foolish. You are not bound by time but we will surely see the cold face of death. But despite our weaknesses and frailties, through a divine partnership with You we are positioned and empowered to do great things with the resources You have put under our management. Like Your Son admonished us, greater things than what He did on earth we will be able to do as we leverage Your almighty power. We are destined to do great things with our lives, our spiritual gifts, and wealth development initiatives. By properly using the little that we have and the infiniteness of thy greatness, we are more than conquerors. We are now economic warriors and change masters!

Amen

The Omni-X Principle

Principle # 2: The Omni-X Principle

"Don't you know that the Lord our God is the everlasting One? Haven't you heard that He always was and always will be? He's the Creator of the universe! He never gets tired. He never gets weary. His understanding and comprehension has no limits. He gives strength to those who are weak and energy to those who are weary." -- Isaiah 40: 28, 29

"Our God lives in heaven and does whatever He wants anywhere on earth." -- Psalm 115:3

"I am the Lord, thy God who is everywhere, the God who is nearby and far away. I see everything and everyone. No one can hide from me. I am everywhere in heaven and on earth." -- Jeremiah 23: 23, 24

One of the best ways to understand and appreciate the power and awesomeness of God is to study astronomy and the architecture of the universe. Once one appreciates the complexity and the vastness of our universal home, the logical leap from the creation of the universe to the acceptance and realization of God's everyday power becomes easier to make.

A study of the physical universe does cause one to pause and take notice. For example, the Solar system in which we (us earthlings) reside contains the Sun and the nine rotating planets (i.e. Mercury, Venus, Earth, Mars, Jupiter, Saturn, Uranus, Neptune, and Pluto). Our Solar system sits within the Milky Way Galaxy, which, by the way, consists of 200 billion stars. Scientists estimate that the Milky Way Galaxy alone is about 100,000 light-years in diameter and about 10,000 light-years thick. (A light-year is the distance that a beam of light can travel within one year. A light-year equals 5,880,000,000,000 miles!) Even more amazing than the intricacy of our galaxy is the fact that scientists estimate that there are over 100 billion other galaxies that share the universe with us. Now just pause for a moment and let this entire reality sink in and marvel at the power, completeness, and absoluteness of God because He made all of this in just six days!

Thus the Omni-X principle is a feeble attempt to wrap our arms around the absoluteness of God. The prefix signifies a combining form meaning all that is often used to describe the completeness of our God. God is the most amazing, awesome, magnificent, marvelous, wonderful, outstanding, and superlative Being in the universe.

First of all, we need to remember that He is omnipotent, which means He has unlimited power and authority over all humanity, all creation, and all matter. The realm of His power transcends the great gulf between the far reaches of the universe down to the minutest detail of atomic structures.

Power is the operative word here. Researching the word power reveals that it is simply the ability to do, or act with strength, might, or force. During the dark and difficult days of the civil rights movement, Dr. Martin Luther King, Jr. was often quoted as saying that power is simply the ability to achieve purpose in the face of resistance. There is nothing or no one in the entire universe that has the power to prevent God from carrying out His agenda. This power is automatically inherited by His children who dwell on this Earth and the heavenly agents that help carry out His plan throughout the universe.

Not only is God all powerful, but He is also omnipresent. In other words, He is present everywhere at the same time. He is in the Nandi District of Kenya East Africa at the same time He is in South Central Los Angeles. He resides on the planet Pluto at the same time He is on the star Alpha Centauri, over 4 light-years away from the sun. God's presence is felt at the lofty heights of Mount Everest, the highest point on Earth, at the same time He can be found at the dark and chilly depths, miles below the surface of the Atlantic and Pacific Oceans.

In addition to His infinite power and pervasive presence, God is omniscient. His mind encompasses all knowledge and understanding from eternity past to eternity future. God knows about every human being that has ever lived upon the planet Earth as well as all beings in undiscovered worlds. According to H. Russell Bernard, University of Florida anthropologists, and Peter D. Killworth, an English physicist, the average American knows 290 people. In their research, what constitutes knowing is that you must remember the person's full name and have had contact with him or her in the last two years. I estimate that as of the year 2004, more than 12 Billion people have passed through life, and what is amazing is that God knows every single one of them by name as well as all the other beings that have existed in the undiscovered worlds of the universe.

His infinite intelligence means that He has complete knowledge, awareness, and understanding. He is the master engineer, doctor, lawyer, nurse, politician, entrepreneur, janitor, astronomer, rocket scientist, dietician, teacher, policeperson, fireperson, chemist, and athlete. He is so smart that none of our problems are too big, too small, or too complicated for God to understand and impart wisdom to and solutions for.

In summary, God has complete, absolute, total, and unequivocal power over the universe. There is nothing in the universe that is greater than He. God's great power triad reveals that He has overcome all foes, all time constraints, all space and distance limitations, and all knowledge and matter frontiers. Those people who are the children of God have inherited this amazing power from God through their Father-child relationship with Him. We are heirs to His mighty fortune, riches, and power. There is nothing that He cannot and will not do for us if we are serving Him, focusing on His Agenda, and living as we ought.

But if God has all of this power and we, His children, have complete access to all who He is and all that He owns, then why aren't we doing greater things on Earth in His name? The reason for our weak response to our inherent greatness is that we persist as a group in "chumpifying" God. In my old neighborhood the word "chump" was used to describe someone who was weak, who lacked conviction, and was devoid of any serious power. Some may view this as overstating the point but keep in mind that we "chumpify" God when we:

• Choose sin over salvation.

• Focus more on the "drama" of life instead of the "dream" of life.

• Fail to take Him at His word.

• Fail to act on His promises.

• Fail to dream beyond our physical and mental limitations and leverage the awesome Omni-Xs of our God!

To avoid falling into this trap, our challenge is to let our dreams match the power of our God. If God is unlimited in scope, it stands to reason that our dreams should be unlimited in scope. If God is all powerful, our wealth dreams should not be limited by the constraints of the immediate. If God is mighty, we too are mighty. When we dream of our Ssese Project, we should remember that we stand on the shoulders of God and, consequently, nothing is impossible for us to achieve.

Tips for Implementing This Ssese Principle in Your Life

1. When looking at your wealth objectives, learn how to first create the future and then work backwards. Make sure that the future goal is big enough and bold enough to keep your interest and spark your passion.

2. Focus on the dream and not the drama. In other words, don't focus on the problems and challenges of this life (the drama). Yes, the drama is real but so is the dream! Put all your wealth creation energies into that place or state that you desire to be in at some future date (the dream).

3. Your wealth creation potential is maximized when you own "stuff" that consistently appreciates in value (e.g. houses, land, limited and diminishing natural resources, etc.)

4. Commit your wealth plans to God and listen carefully to His instructions.

A Prayer for the Wealthy Minded

Dear Yahweh (Jehovah in English – "I AM"):

Men marvel at Your power, awesomeness, majesty, and might. Yet, if we're honest, we have to wonder, for what is man that Thou art so mindful of him? Why does an almighty God who owns and manages the entire universe, care so much about lowly, sinful creatures, who inhabit such a small and insignificant planet buried in the cosmos? One day we will learn the answer to that question, but, until then, teach me how to leverage the wonders and power of Your might that

I might set the proper financial goals and rely upon Your complete and generous resources to reach them.

Amen

Principle # 3: Principle of Ownership

"The Earth is the Lord's and everything in it; the world and all who live here are His. For He formed it in the middle of the waters and set the boundaries and depths of the seas." -- Psalm 24: 1-2

When I was a child, my grandfather and grandmother Curry were the cornerstones of our extended family unit. Grandmother Curry liked to sing the old songs that were sung by her parents and by many of our ancestors. One song she sang, especially during times of upheaval, confusion, chaos, and utter hopelessness, was a song entitled "He's Got the Whole World in His Hands." This particular song celebrated the fact that God owned the entire world and all that was in it.

Those times were especially difficult for my family. It was during the mid-1960s when my family was experiencing one of its darkest periods. First of all, there was turmoil in the family. Momma and Daddy weren't getting along very well. Daddy had a hard time covering our monthly living expenses because he had more expenses than he had work. His attempts to try and drink his problems away didn't help matters much either.

As the Vietnam War began reaching its greatest intensity, our dear Uncle Sam took not one, not two but three of my older brothers to fight in that unjust war in Southeast Asia. Despite her Herculean effort to wear a smile on her face and give the outside world the impression that all was well, Momma finally succumbed to all the pressure and reluctantly turned to alcohol as a means of relieving the pain and hurt that she was going through. For many tortuous years, alcohol became her best friend and most ardent supporter. It also almost single handedly destroyed our family.

It was during these difficult and uncertain times that the leadership, love, and prayers of my grandparents became so crucial to our long-term survival. My grandparents not only provided us food and clothing during this time but more importantly they provided us the spiritual uplifting that was so badly needed. Grandmother especially would minister to us through song. The songs she sang reminded us that the current conditions that we were forced to live under were not permanent or final. Her song reminded us that there was someone who loved us with an infinite love and who owned the universe, and would eventually move on our situation in such a way that our pain and suffering would be relieved. Grandfather Curry, who was so strong and wise, often whispered in my ear whenever we had a quiet moment together, "Son, trouble don't last always."

"But Grand Daddy, What Does God Really Own?"

Although my grandfather assured me that God owned everything, to understand this point adequately, it is important to recognize that, as I discussed earlier, there are two kingdoms in our world. The two kingdoms are not defined by race, gender, ethnicity, economic status, or geographical location. Instead they are broken into the Kingdom of God and the kingdom of Satan. In each kingdom there are four types of resources that can be used at the King's discretion. These resources are our time, our talent, our treasures (the stuff of life) and our temple (the human body).

The underlying power of this principle is that The Earth and every thing in it belongs to God. This world, our Universe and all who live here are His. For God formed it in the middle of the waters and set the boundaries and depths of the seas. What is interesting and fascinating is that God ultimately owns all things "owned" by those who reside in Satan's kingdom as well as those who reside in the Kingdom of God. While Satan is restricted to only using the resources in his kingdom, God is able to "crossover" and use the resources in Satan's kingdom as well as those resources residing in the Kingdom of God.

The second awesome reality about God's power of ownership is the real estate or just the amount that He owns. For example, if we tried to define and estimate the size of God's universe our feeble minds would only be able to estimate the vastness of God's creation. The distance from one end of our solar system to the other is approximately 8 billion miles. Traveling at 60 miles per hour, it would take a traveler 75 years to travel from one end of the system to the other.

Our Father not only owns the Earth and its galaxy the Milky Way, but He also owns the star Alpha Centauri in the Centaurus Constellation, which is four light-years away. Beyond the star Alpha Centauri, he also holds eternal rights to the star Canopus, which dwells in the Carina Constellation and which is some 650 light-years away from the Earth!

If God owns so much and is in charge of everything and if He loves us like He does, there is nothing that He can't perform in our favor. There is nothing that our finite minds can conceive that does not belong to God. Whether it is money, gold, silver, real estate, technology, machinery, or good health, God owns it all, so He has the power and the authority to give it away to whomever He pleases. That is why it is paramount that we never let the constraints of our physical reality dictate to us the size and enormity of our dreams and aspirations. It is important to start small but think big because our Father has the power and might to do any and all things that He desires. We have access to the greatest power in the Universe; all we have to do is understand what He expects from us, do it, and make our wishes known to Him. He is capable, able, and willing.

Tips for Implementing This Ssese Principle in Your Life

1. Nothing in the universe is off limits to you because it is all owned by God. God is your Father, and thus you are a legitimate owner of all that belongs to Him.

2. God not only owns all the resources under the management of godly people but He also owns all resources that are currently under the management of ungodly people. You are unrestricted in where you mine for wealth opportunities. Consequently, you have a legitimate right to the wealth that is currently under the management of the ungodly.

3. Learn to balance present material gain with eternal riches.

4. There is power in knowing the owners' of "stuff." Therefore expand your opportunities to get to know people who own/control lots of "stuff." Commit to get to know them in a very sincere and intimate way and not just superficially. It is not necessarily who you know that is important but how "well" you know them.

A Prayer for the Wealthy Minded

Dear Jehovah Jireh ("I AM" + Provider):

I am so glad You are my Father and that You're very wealthy and own everything in the universe. Because You own so much, I realize that I don't have to ever accept poverty as a way of life. I may experience poverty but I am not poor, because I belong to You. I may experience riches and wealth but it all belongs to You. Remind me that all I have to do is stay true to You, plan for my life, follow

Your lead, and accept the fact that You, in Your infinite wisdom, will provide all that I need, a portion of what I want, and even some of what I desire according to Your riches in glory.

Amen

Principle # 4: The Principle of Love

"For God loved the world so much that He freely gave His only Son to come here and die, that whoever believes in Him will not perish but will be given eternal life. God didn't send His Son to the world to condemn people, but to forgive them and save them." -- John 3:16, 17

"What do you mean I have to get out the car, Moses?" I yelled at the top of my voice. The night was bitterly cold, the air was clear, and the streetlights cast a shadow over my face, hiding the anger and confusion I felt over Moses' instructions for me to get out of his car. Our dear friend, Raphael, had just gotten "banked" (street jargon for being attacked and assaulted by a gang of people) and the five of us were speeding to the place where the attack occurred so that we could administer "street justice" on those who hurt our friend and brother. Moses yelled out at me again, "Get out the car, college boy! We have some business to take care of and you don't need to be mixed up in the trouble we're about to get into. You're on your way to college and you can't allow what's about to go down to mess you up. So go back home. We'll meet you back on the corner."

As Jimmy nudged me out the car, I heard the door slam shut as the car sped through the green light and turned left on Biddle Street. As I stood in the middle of the dark, damp street, I couldn't help but worry about what trouble my friends were about to get into. Cold and still angry at Moses for putting me out of the car, I walked to the corner and caught the #28 Bus to head home before my mother got home from working her second job.

By the time I got home later that evening, word had gotten back that my friend Moses and the rest of my buddies in the car had been successful at carrying out their mission but were unsuccessful at getting away from the scene of the incident. All four of my childhood friends had been arrested as a result of their actions.

Not a day goes by that I don't think about this experience and what would have happened to me and my life if Moses had not demanded that I get out the car that particular night. Moses has since passed away, but the love and concern he showed for me that night I will never forget.

The love that had Moses showed me that night, while noble and sincere, is nothing in comparison to the love that God has for us every day. God truly is love. He loved us so much that He sacrificed His only begotten Son so that whoever believed in Him would not perish but would enjoy the gift of eternal life. His nature, His law, is love. It ever has been; it ever will be. "The high and lofty One that inhabiteth eternity, whose ways are everlasting, changeth not. With Him is no variableness, neither shadow of turning." (Isaiah 57:15; Habakkuk 3:6; James 1:17) Every manifestation of creative power is an expression of infinite love. The sovereignty of God involves fullness of blessing to all created beings.

His most powerful feeling towards us is the love that He showers upon us. God provided the ultimate sign of love when He allowed His only begotten Son, Jesus Christ, to exchange Christ's robe of righteousness for our robes of sin and iniquity and seal Himself with the flesh of humanity, walk this earth as a man walks it, and ultimately allow Him to be butchered at the hands of evil men.

Beyond the cross God also shows His love for us by providing us food to eat, water to drink, clothes to wear, bodies that function, shelter against the elements, a brain that is more powerful than any super computer, and the ability to dream things that are not and say with confidence and passion, Why not?

God's love for us is so awesome that He waits our seeking of Him to discuss in earnest the desires of our heart. It is that love that allows men and women to dream and believe in a big time way. Because God loves us, we are not afraid to take prudent risks and expect Him to be there for us and to bless us at the appropriate time.

Loving Those Who Hate And Despise Us

There are often times in our efforts to build businesses and create wealth, that we are forced to interface with people who are mean or disrespectful, and who have disdain for us. Their dislike for us might be based upon our race, ethnicity, gender or physical appearance or they might be just plain old mean people. The fact of the matter is that you can only build wealth working with and through people. It is extremely difficult and just about impossible to create wealth alone. Therefore it becomes essential that you learn to love those (loving them makes it easier to like and work with them) who hate and despise us. Hate is a heavy burden to shoulder. Let someone else carry that load.

How Is It Possible to Love Those Who Hate Us?

God gives us clear directions on how we are to love those who hate us. He says in His word: "But show love for your enemies by doing nice things for them. Don't do good in order to get something back from them. You'll be rewarded for what you do because you're the children of God. He's kind and gracious even to the most ungrateful and wicked." -- Luke 6:35

If you find it very difficult to love your enemies and have a hard time working with certain people to create wealth, remember these points:

- God loves them just as much as He loves you. They are just as much a part of His creation as you and I are. We are no greater or no worse than they. God may not like their behavior but He loves them because God is love.

- There is a part of God that lives in them as well as in you and me. Although some people chose not to be a part of the Kingdom of God, a part of God's Spirit still resides in them as long as they draw breath. Because there is a part of God in them, when loving them we focus on that part of them that most looks like God.

- As we strive to love them our commitment to love them enhances and strengthens our relationship with God. As Dr. Martin Luther King Jr. taught the civil rights workers to love those who hated them and the workers began to live out this creed, they became stronger as their enemies became weaker. Their strength enhancement was not of themselves but was of God.

- Whenever we start thinking about how terrible our enemies might be, we should take a look in the mirror and take a close look at ourselves. If we're honest, we will probably find some things about ourselves that others might not find so attractive. This critical self-discernment helps us to not think more of ourselves then we ought to.

Tips for Implementing This Ssese Principle in Your Life

1. God loves you more than you can comprehend, therefore, He is willing to do anything for you as long as it is within His will and plan for your life. God believes in your dreams because He gave them to you and He will work in partnership with you to make them come true. Since His plan for your life is "incrementally" revealed to you over time, push the envelope of possibility and think big. Start small, but think big!

2. God requires that we love others as much as we love ourselves. This rule requires that whatever wealth you build serves to not only benefit you but others around you. Ultimately the wealth should be used as an enabler to fortify and expand the Kingdom of God.

3. When we love, we sacrifice. When we love, we forgive. When we love we recognize that someone could be your enemy today but your business partner tomorrow.

4. Love for God means we put nothing before Him. If we violate a Godly principle, that means we value the blessing more than we do the One who blessed us.

5. Love for ourselves means that whatever we do in life we do with the utmost intensity, seriousness, passion, and focus on excellence. We recognize that we represent God in everything we do. We work, study, and practice to be the best we can be at what we do.

6. Love for our community means that we pursue wealth creation strategies that not only benefit us individually but also benefit us collectively and corporately. We make an effort to educate and mentor those who may not be as "wealth wise" as we are.

7. Because you do what you love to do, your proficiency in that area expands beyond your imagination and revenue flows from your efforts will eventually flow into your coffers.

8. Because of love, you consistently remain faithful in your tithes and offerings because this is a tangible way of showing your trust in and love for God. God then recognizes your faith and uses it as an actuator that opens the windows of heaven to you and pours out more blessings that you are able to absorb.

A Prayer for the Wealthy Minded

Dear Jehovah Rophe ("I AM" + Healer):

Not a day goes by that you don't reveal the wonderful and amazing love that you have for humanity. We see your love in the rising of the sun. We hear your love in the churning of the ocean waves. We feel your love in the sureness of the rhythm of our heart beats. Teach us that, like a loving Father, you desire to give us the desires and wishes of our hearts. Your love lifts and takes us higher and higher and your blessings include financial and wealth creation opportunities that we don't deserve, haven't earned, but yet we receive. Remind us that the love you show us should be reflected in the love that we show humanity, as we use our resources to continue the work of Christ until He returns.

Principle # 5: The Principle of Wealth Transfer

"A good man leaveth an inheritance to his children's children: and the wealth of the sinner is laid up for the just." -- Proverbs 13:22

"They also had gone to the Egyptians asking for their back pay and for support with silver, gold and articles of clothing. The Lord gave His people favor in the eyes of the Egyptians and the children of Israel received more than they had asked for. So the Israelites took with them much of the wealth of Egypt." -- Exodus 12: 35-36

Steve was furious. "How could this be? We are clearly better qualified for this biometrics contract with the Department of Army. Yet they award the contract to a company that has a reputation for cutthroat marketing tactics and that has a questionable performance history with large biometric installations. These guys are bad news yet they end up walking away with the prize.

This whole episode leaves a bad taste in my mouth. It seems like us good guys just can't win!"

Steve, a devoted Christian, was a Vietnam veteran and had built up an impeccable reputation in the biometric engineering field. He had invested a lot of resources working with the customer on complex security problems and had even forsaken maximizing his profits with that customer, instead choosing to be honest and straightforward. Now he wondered what that honesty and integrity achieved for him.

Monday morning came too soon for Steve because it meant he would have to clean out the proposal room (they called it the war room) and file away all of the paper, charts, proposal drafts, and other traces of their valiant but unrewarded efforts to win the contract. As Steve was tearing down the last flip chart from off of the wall the intercom system in Steve's office sounded out. "Steve, Ms. Johnson, the contracting officer for the Department of Army, is holding for you on line 15."

Steve wondered to himself, "Why in the world is she calling me? She already informed me that we were not awarded the contract. What else could she possibly want?" "Hello Steve, this is Ms. Johnson from the Army. I am calling you to inform you that the company that was awarded the contract just filed bankruptcy and they are no longer able to perform. Since your firm had the second highest score during the proposal evaluations, we would like to award your firm the contract."

Steve could not believe what he was hearing but he had learned as a young boy to always count your blessings, even when some times you don't understand them. "Thank you, Ms. Johnson. You just made my day." As Steve confirmed with Ms. Johnson the specifics signing the contracts, he thought, "Maybe, just maybe, the good guys do win every now and then!"

Make no mistake about it, God owns the entire Earth and all who are within it. But because Satan has introduced sin into the world and desires to establish his own kingdom to rival God's Kingdom, there are those who have chosen to join the kingdom of Satan and turn their back on God. What is interesting about God's long-term strategy for dealing with the destruction of Satan and his followers is that he allows the enemy to control (temporarily) a certain amount of physical, intellectual, and spiritual resources.

Many of us know people who are wealthy, talented, famous, and powerful but who do not know or have an interest in knowing God. Satan has influenced humankind since the days of Adam and Eve and has been allowed to establish his kingdom. These people exert great influence in business, government, universities, and other societal institutions. Satan's end-time deceptions persuade "those who are to perish, because they refused to love the truth and so be saved." God permits Satan to unveil his most insidious delusions, "to make them believe what is false, so that all may be condemned who did not believe the truth but had pleasure in unrighteousness." (2 Thessalonians 2:10, 11)

One thing I have learned about God is that He does have a sense of humor and a keen sense of timing. As humanity moves closer and closer to the final chapters of its earthly existence, God will begin to accelerate the transfer of earthly wealth and riches into the control of His faithful and anointed people. As we move closer to the day when Jesus Christ will return for His second (and next to final) advent, God will require that increasing amounts of wealth reside in the hands and under the control of His people. These increased resources are necessary so that there will be sufficient earthly wealth for soldiers of God around the world to carry out their mission and to proclaim to the world one last time the cosmic warning of the three angel's message that is heralded in the book of Revelation.

First Angel (Rev. 14:6): "...Fear God and give him glory, for the hour of his judgment has come; and worship Him who made heaven and earth, the sea and the fountains of water."

Second Angel (Rev. 14:8): "...Fallen, fallen is Babylon [i.e. a symbol of the vast community of people who, like Babylon of old, were to blaspheme God and persecute the true saints] the great, she who made all nations drink the wine of her pure passion."

Third Angel (Rev. 14: 9-12): "And another angel, a third, followed them, saying with a loud voice, "If any one worships the beast and its image, and receives a mark on his forehead or on his hand, he also shall drink the wine of God's wrath, poured unmixed into the cup of his anger, and he shall be tormented with fire and sulphur in the presence of the holy angels and in the presence of the Lamb. And the smoke of their torment goes up for ever and ever; and they have no rest, day or night, these worshipers of the beast and its image, and whoever receives the mark of its name. Here is a call for the endurance of the saints, those who keep the commandments of God and the faith of Jesus."

This principle of wealth transfer from the ungodly to the godly is not new or modern. In fact throughout the history of the church on this earth God has provided his church the resources it requires to carry out His divine plan. For example, after being slaves for more than four hundred years, the children of Israel walked out of the land of Egypt as millionaires. At the command of God, before the Jews left Egypt they approached the Egyptians and requested that they pay them for all of their labor and the children of Israel took with them most of the wealth of Egypt.

I have often wondered how the children of Israel, having been in bondage for more than four centuries, were able to quickly accrue so much wealth in such a short period of time. I have also been puzzled about the fact that Pharaoh, who had witnessed first hand all of the amazing miracles and show of power that God had displayed in Egypt on behalf of His children, was so foolish as to pursue the Jews into the Red Sea. This fact is especially incredulous after Pharaoh must have seen the great walls of water that God swelled up to prepare a dry passageway of escape into the promise land.

The answer to my astonishment at Pharaoh's decision to pursue the Jews is found in the book of Exodus 15:9: "The enemy said, 'I will pursue them and catch them. I will draw the sword and force them to return. I will recover the wealth I gave them and take it all back.'" In other words, Pharaoh allowed his greed to overcome his common sense and logic because he realized he had been fooled by the Jews and desired to reclaim the wealth of his nation.

This principle highlights the fact that God, at the proper time, will begin transferring the wealth and riches of the ungodly into the capable hands of the godly. The godly people must first work with God to increase their competence and "spiritual intelligence" in order to receive this wealth from God. Once received from God, the wealth is not only to be used to make one's life more productive but it should be used to help others who are less fortunate and, ultimately used to enhance the Kingdom of God.

What Determines the Rate of Wealth Transfer in Our Lives

When I deliver my workshop on "Creating Wealth: From the Inside Out," I am often asked, "What determines the rate of wealth transfer into my life?" Of course, there is no perfect answer to this question. Neither is God prepared to make all Christians filthy wealthy although some will come to manage large quantities of wealth. But while there is no "crystal ball" on this matter there are some factors that I have seen from anecdotal observation that do seem to impact the rate of transfer. The four factors that I have observed are:

• Our spiritual capacity to receive the blessings and wealth that God would put under our management. God will not transfer wealth to us if He knows that our having it would pull us further away from Him and the plan that He has for our lives. I remember during the 1980s trying valiantly to purchase a multimillion-dollar manufacturing business in Newark, New Jersey. My partners and I mortgaged our homes and took all of our savings to invest in this deal. Not a day went by that I didn't pray to God to make this deal happen. I even contemplated fasting to really get God's attention. We knew that once the deal closed that we would enjoy significant increases in our income, prestige, fame, and power. Just the sheer size of the transaction at that time would have caught the attention of most of the media and the business world. My partners and I would have become famous over night. But giving that business to me was not in God's plans and the deal died a sudden, painful death. At the time, I was devastated, bitter, angry, and broke.

But now, 15 years later, I look back on that situation and thank God that He in His infinite wisdom chose not to permit the deal to close. I know now that if I had become owner of that company at that point in my spiritual maturity, I would have likely lost my soul. My spiritual capacity was still small and limited, and I would have allowed the success to go to my head and, like so many others, would have probably ended up turning my back on God.

• Our commitment to Christ and His Kingdom agenda. Make no mistake, Christ's second coming is sooner than we anticipate. We are in the period called Pre-Advent Judgement. Christ has moved to the Most Holy Place of the Heavenly Sanctuary. Therefore all of our earthly resources are to be dedicated to strengthening the saints of God and expanding the Kingdom throughout the world. Our commitment to the tenets of this Kingdom agenda will partially determine our rate of transfer.

• The role that you play in the Kingdom agenda will determine the amount and velocity of wealth transfer. All believers are of the family of God and make up the body of Christ. Each of us plays a unique role and assumes a special aspect of the body of Christ. Therefore because we assume different responsibilities we require different skills and resources to be successful in the work God has planned for our lives. This fact also means that we can expect different amounts of wealth than others. God will transfer the amount of wealth that we need to complete the spiritual mission for our lives.

• Our motivation for desiring the wealth in the first place will dictate the amount and velocity of wealth transfer that we experience. When I was a younger man, I harbored this insatiable desire to be rich. I had been raised a poor child in the projects of Baltimore City but had the opportunity to attend schools where I was interfacing with children of the rich and well-to-do. I resented the fact that while my parents had to work, beg, and borrow to accumulate just enough resources for my brothers and me to survive, my affluent peers had the finest of all the nice things that America has to offer – fine clothes, expensive cars, large homes, extravagant vacations, business holdings, power, and societal status. As I studied their family structures and financial characteristics my internal desire for riches and wealth swelled within me. While nice homes, cars, and affluence have their place and nothing is wrong with these objects within themselves, if they are the end that justifies the means, then this approach to wealth will lead to ruin and emptiness. However, if our motivation for wealth is so that the Kingdom of God prospers and becomes wealthier, then our strategy will likely be in harmony with the will of God, we prove our trustworthiness to God, and He then opens up the store room of heaven to shower the proper amount of resources upon us.

Tips for Implementing This Ssese Principle in Your Life

1. God has allowed ungodly people to become managers of much of the world's wealth. Part of the reason might be that many of God's people have not shown themselves ready to receive and "manage" the enormous amounts of wealth God is ready to transfer to His people.

2. Ungodly people don't understand that they don't really own their assets but that God has allowed these assets to come under their control to achieve His holy purposes. Thus, the ungodly when their minds become poisoned with the world's wealth they become cocky, arrogant, foolish, sloppy, and prime candidates for rapid wealth transfer.

3. God begins transferring wealth once He is comfortable that we are spiritually mature enough to receive and manage it.

4. It is important to mark out your territory. You want to be close enough to the ungodly that when its time to transfer that you're the likely candidate. This fact means you can't hide yourself away but instead you must socialize with and get to know the ungodly. By being "in the world" and "not of the world" we have greater opportunities to convert non-believers and absorb the wealth of those who chose to turn their backs on God. This approach does not suggest that we become like them but we should never segregate ourselves from them.

5. How do we show God that we're ready to receive the transfer? We show Him by managing the little wealth that we have now extremely well. Conduct a self-analysis and ask yourself: How well are you managing the treasure that you have now? How well do you manage your health? Is your time properly allocated? When we show God that we can be trusted with a little, then He will begin transferring to us a lot.

6. God will transfer only as much wealth as He knows that you can handle. God would rather you be not so wealthy on Earth and share eternity with Him than to be rich on Earth and be lost for eternity. Our capacity for receiving and managing wealth is a function of the individual; consequently the amount of wealth put under our management will be different. This is why God warns us about the dangers of covetousness because of our natural tendency to be jealous about what others have.

7. Our goal in mastering this principle should be to reach that level between extreme poverty and crazy wealth so that on one

hand we don't curse God for our poverty and on the other hand, we don't forget about Him because we have so much.

A Prayer for the Wealthy Minded

Dear Jehovah Nissi ["I AM" + A Banner (victory)]

Too many times, our enemies and the ungodly of this earth laugh at and ridicule Your children because while the ungodly seem to have plenty, sometimes Your children seem to struggle and are often forced to go without. In too many situations it does seem like evil men prosper while good men suffer. We recognize and accept the fact that if we are here to serve You, then suffering and struggle will become one of our lifelong companions. But in these times of spiritual challenge, please bring back to our remembrance that You are the greatest Power in the universe, that Your love for us is infinite, and that, in due season when we have shown ourselves prepared, You will gladly transfer all of the wealth that we need. From the ledger of the evil to the ledger of thy people, you will swiftly shift more time, enhanced talents, appropriate amount of treasures, and good health. Those of us who keep the faith, who maintain the commandments of God and the testimony of Jesus Christ, who finish their course, and who never, ever give up, will eat freely from the tree of life which You have prepared since the foundations of the earth were laid.

Amen

Principle # 6: The Principle of the Giving Sequence

"Don't worry about what to eat or what to drink or what to wear. These are the priorities of the world. Remember, your heavenly Father knows that you need food and clothes. So make God's Kingdom and His righteousness first in your life, and all the other things will be given to you as you need them." -- Mathew 6:31-33

"Give, and it shall be given unto you; good measure, pressed down, and shaken together, and running over, shall men give into your bosom. For with the same measure that ye mete withal it shall be measured to you again." -- Luke 6:38

Cora was frustrated that after 18 months of aggressive marketing to a very strategic customer, she seemed no closer to closing the sale than she did over a year and a half ago. "Am I not getting any business because I'm a women-owned business or because I'm Latino?" she often wondered when she had a quiet moment.

One day as she was contemplating how she would keep her business afloat, she got a phone call from Lisa Gonzales, a contracts administrator with the customer that she had been courting for business for so long. "Cora, we finally have an opportunity that was tailor made for your firm. Unfortunately, the contract still needs to be approved by the Board of Estimates before we can cut you a purchase order but due to a federal mandate, we are required to start the work immediately. I assure you that the approval by the board is simply a formality and you will get paid," Lisa assured Cora.

Cora was on the horns of a major dilemma. Should she accept and begin the work even though the contract had not been signed? She recalled hearing horror stories about companies who began projects before a formal contract had been signed and ended up losing money when it was determined that the contract would not be approved as was promised. Her only other option was to reject the opportunity and miss out on this once-in-a-life-time chance to get her foot in the door with a well sought after client.

After an intimate, earnest, and honest discussion with God, Cora opted to begin working immediately on the contract. Shortly thereafter, the Board of Estimates approved the contract and Cora's company was formally awarded the work. As it turned out, this customer became one of her most loyal and financially lucrative customers. Lisa would later comment to Cora, "People here really appreciated your willingness to work with us when we were in a jam. You really built up a tremendous amount of goodwill within our organization. Our staff really appreciates that you were willing to give before you received." Years earlier, our beloved former president, John Fitzgerald Kennedy, challenged America during one of its most challenging periods. In his inaugural address the president admonished his fellow Americans when he said: "Ask not, what your country can do for you. Instead ask what you can do for your country!"

What President Kennedy was conveying to the American people was that for America to become a truly great nation, all of us must focus more on what we can give to one another, our community, and thus our nation instead of only thinking of our individual needs. He may have also been reminding us that we will all be rewarded in the long term if we adopt the give first and be rewarded later model that this principle attempts to articulate.

What Is the Proper Sequence of Giving to Build Wealth?

Whatever vision President Kennedy was ultimately trying to convey to the nation, the sad fact is that in our world today most people believe that they should get first and then maybe they will consider giving. Their philosophy in life is "I got mine, now you go get yours!" However, this philosophy of getting first and giving later is contrary to the word of God as well as to the principles of success.

Submit to God First

To build long-term success and a wealth foundation that is sustainable and enjoyable, we must learn that our first submittal is to God. Make no mistake about it. You are free to go out and build wealth without God. There are many examples in the world today of people who are wealthy but ungodly. The difference, I believe, between the ungodly wealthy and the godly wealthy is that the godly wealthy invest over a longer time period. While they diligently invest during their 70-plus years (maybe) that they reside on this Earth, they just as diligently invest in the eternity to come. Since the godly tend to have a mission for their wealth, they tend to enjoy their life to its fullest. They take comfort in knowing that when they close their eyes in death they will open them and look upon the wonderful face of Jesus Christ and assist Him in the management of the universe for eons and eons. What a comfort and confidence this reality provides the battle worn saints of God.

The godly ones who forget or refuse to first submit themselves to God before starting the journey of wealth creation and business success provide a point of vulnerability at which the evil one and his demons are able to rush into our inner thoughts and heart and construct portals of greed, covetousness, and selfishness. When we allow this to happen, we end up with possibly some level of financial success, but we have no foundation, no direction, no purpose, and we lose out on the blessings that God had in store for us.

Jim was a man who while seemingly successful on the outside had experienced the frustration and uncertainty that comes from not first submitting ourselves to God. By all the measures that society seems to use to gauge worldly success, Jim was a man who was on a fast track to jet to the top. First, he had the Ivy League credentials and stellar educational pedigree. On top of that he was young, good-looking, likeable, social, intelligent, and had a lovely wife and family. What most people didn't realize though was that while everything looked great on the surface, Jim was struggling personally and financially. While Jim's company provided a great service and was well respected within the industry in which he worked, like so many other small businesses, his company had been terribly undercapitalized and consequently regularly faced severe cash flow problems. The cash flow problems became so pervasive and so intense that it began to threaten the very survival of his company.

What made Jim's situation even direr was the fact that his company went into a rut at the same time cash flow began to dry up. Many of his revenue streams began to either dry up or were reduced to a trickle. Although Jim and his capable staff worked diligently to build new revenue streams by expanding their services with existing customers while reaching out to provide existing services to new customers, every attempt they made to realize these new opportunities failed. It seemed that every appointment they made with a customer was cancelled, every proposal written was rejected, and every application for new lines of credits with both banks and suppliers were not approved.

Jim, who was a proud believer, began to lose his confidence and balance as a business man. It got to a point that everyday, after Jim's staff had left for the day, Jim would confine himself to the solitude of his office and weep bitterly out of frustration, anger, and concern for the future. Even though Jim was seeking God everyday through prayer, it appeared to Jim that God had shut up His ears to his urgent pleas and refused to answer Jim's calls for help.

One night, as Jim was driving home from the office, he realized that he had reached his psychological and spiritual limits. Without thought, he began to weep uncontrollably. He began beating on the dashboard and screaming and yelling at God. Careful to not cross the line of disrespect, Jim asked God repeatedly, "Father, why won't you help me? Why? Why? I am trying to be a good man, I am trying to live right, and I attend church and faithfully give my tithe and offering! Yet, you're not helping me! Why?"

As the night drew on and Jim's temper and tears began to subside, Jim pulled into the driveway of his home. As he sat there trying vainly to regain his composure before he faced his lovely wife, Jim recalled having a peace and serenity come over him that dramatically contrasted his feelings from just a few minutes ago. In that peaceful moment God spoke to Jim and reminded him

that although Jim was going "through the motions" of having a relationship with God, the fact was, that Jim had not really "submitted" his life to God completely and fully. God later impressed on Jim that until he fully surrendered and submitted all aspects of his life to Him, that it would be fruitless for Jim to try to serve God in any meaningful way. Jim heard God that night and that "conversation" completely changed his life.

Jim's "conversation" with God reminded him and should remind us that once we submit our lives to God that we are not to worry about what we to eat or what to drink or what to wear. God knows what we need and has promised to make provisions for us. What God wants us to do is to first submit ourselves to Him and His wishes and plans for our lives. If we make Him first in our lives then all of the other things that we need will be given to us, as we need them. Once we give ourselves to God first He will then provide us the time, talent, temple (physical health), and treasure (money and assets) to complete the mission that He has designed for our lives.

Tips for Implementing This Ssese Principle in Your Life

1. God gives us four distinct assets that can be used to create wealth – time, talent, temple (physical health) and treasure (money and assets). Therefore, God gave to us before He got anything in return. He stepped out on faith that we would respond to His giving, especially the ultimate gift He gave when he sacrificed His only begotten Son – the gift of eternal life.

2. Be obedient to God and faithfully and consistently give your tithes and offerings to the Kingdom of God to fund His earthly government. God reminds us in the book of Malachi that the tithe (10% of your pretax earnings, your first fruit) belongs to Him. When we fail to give it we are in fact stealing from God, which is not very smart. The amount of offering that we give is up to us. God does not give us a specific percentage in this case. However a rule of thumb I recommend is to give a percentage

that is commensurate with the amount of blessings that God has given you over that time period. Remember to give according to your blessings or God will distribute your blessings according to your giving!

3. Develop a "giving attitude" instead of a "receiving attitude." Giving first makes it possible for you to use leverage in accumulating wealth at an accelerated pace.

4. If you don't invest up front, then you have almost a zero chance of winning. Yes, you could win the lottery but winning a lottery violates the principles of God and will ultimately violate the individual.

5. Don't make the mistake of waiting until the "right time" before you decide to give to the environment that you compete in. Live by this motto: "Give wherever you are, whatever you have, and right now!" The sooner you give the quicker you begin to accrue the deposits of wealth opportunities.

6. Giving first helps build a deep reservoir of goodwill between you and the recipient of your giving. Goodwill makes it easier to gain people's respect and admiration. Respect makes it easier for people to like you. If you're liked then people will go out of their way to assist you in your wealth creation projects. Remember, people do business with people that they like.

7. Work on developing a "giving mentality" instead of a "receiving mentality." Force yourself to take the first step even if you're uncomfortable doing it. The more you give first the more comfortable you become with the process.

A Prayer for the Wealthy Minded

Dear Jehovah Mekadesh ("I AM" + A Sanctifier):

You provided the perfect model depicting the proper sequence of giving when You sacrificed your Son, Jesus Christ. You allowed us to exchange our robe of sin and iniquity for Christ's robe of holiness and righteousness. Teach me that like Christ, I must willingly give of myself, despite what the world might say. Remind me that as I give of my time, talent, treasure, temple, and tithes, that my reward will always far exceed what I put in and surpass my greatest expectations.

Amen

Principle # 7: The Principle of Sowing & Reaping

"Beloved I wish above all things that thou mayest prosper and be in health, even as they soul prospereth." -- 3 John 1:2

"Humility and respect for God will bring riches, honor and a happy life." --Proverbs 22:4

"Train a child in the way he ought to live, and he'll remember it even when he's old." -- Proverbs 22:6

"He who sows iniquity will reap sorrow, and his oppression of others will finally come to an end. A generous man will himself be blessed because he shares his food with the poor." -- Proverbs 22: 8-9

"Carolyn, I understand why your business has not grown as fast as it should have. You spend so much time trying to help others in business that you don't have anytime left for your own business!" Omar blurted out to her as they enjoyed a low-carbohydrate lunch at the downtown diner. Omar was really a good friend who really cared for Carolyn. As he sat across from her carving up his lettuce, tomatoes and broiled chicken, his eyes searched hers as he attempted to advise her on how to jump-start her business again.

Carolyn had invited Omar to lunch because she had been trying to survive through yet another recession and was seeking encouragement and advice. Omar knew that Carolyn was exceptionally bright but it concerned him that ever since she started publishing books on entrepreneurship, people began soliciting advice and guidance, which she freely gave, often times to the detriment of her own struggling enterprise.

Carolyn had started her company ten years ago. She was an accomplished and outstanding scientist in the field of Biotech Engineering and decided, after working many years in research at the National Institutes of Health, to become an entrepreneur and launch her own consulting firm. She had earned her degree in Engineering from the University of Pennsylvania and her Masters in Engineering from the Massachusetts Institute of Technology. Carolyn had published and co-published many papers before she started writing on her own about the challenges women entrepreneurs face and successful strategies they can implement to overcome the sexism and cronyism that was so prevalent in her industry.

As she signaled for the waiter to take her plate away Carolyn sheepishly responded to Omar, "I know you're right. There are just so many of us who are struggling in business that I feel it is my duty to assist those who are in need of support and direction. In a way, I feel like it is my ministry. It seems like it is a special little project that God has assigned to me in this space and time because even though we usually start out talking about business we often end up talking about God." As he finally understood what was driving Carolyn, Omar nodded, in a way giving her his reluctant but implicit endorsement.

Carolyn continued, "This may be hard to understand, Omar, but I perceive myself as sowing seeds of success among my peers. Some of these seeds will lay deep roots and bring forth great business, material, and spiritual success, other seeds will no doubt fail to find a nurturing and receptive environment and will simply whither away. I believe that whatever success these people realize I will ultimately share in it to varying degrees."

A year passed before Carolyn and Omar saw one another again. Having just returned from a business trip to South Africa, Omar anxiously called Carolyn to see how things were going in her business. When Omar dialed her number he immediately didn't recognize the voice on the other end of the phone. "Good morning, you have reached the offices of BioLink Consulting Group. How may I assist you?" a woman with a British sounding accent responded. Somewhat surprised by the unfamiliar voice, Omar said, "May I please speak with Carolyn." The receptionist responded, "Of course you can sir, I will connect you to her extension."

When Carolyn picked up the phone, Omar could immediately sense the excitement and energy in her warm and caring voice. "Carolyn, this is Omar. How in the world are you?" Carolyn responded, "Omar, I am doing fantastic! Since I last met with you, so much has happened with my business. The Lord has blessed us so much and we are growing like crazy. What's amazing about it all is that almost all of our business opportunities are coming from people that we don't even know!" "What do you mean people you don't even know?" Omar incredulously asked. "Well, you know all of those people that I had been advising and guiding on their businesses? Some of them have really become successful and they in turn have invited me into business deals as their partner. Others have referred me to other potential partners and customers. We have tripled our customer base in less than a year. God is truly amazing. I give Him all of the honor and glory for this blessing." Omar listened intently as Carolyn went on to share even more details of how she had been blessed. When she was finished sharing, Omar smiled to himself and said, "Carolyn, it seems like your strategy of sowing and reaping really is paying off. Maybe I need to rethink my business strategy."

Sowing means to scatter, implant, introduce, or disseminate seed for growth. Reaping means to get a return, recompense, or result from the seeds that were planted. People often confuse what the two actions mean and the order in which they must be followed. Like in the recent examples of Enron, WorldCom, and others, business leaders have pursued a 'scorched earth" approach to the building of their businesses by plundering the assets of their corporations and paying themselves handsomely in the process. So many people's lives have been ruined because these so called business leaders have decided to reap without having to sow. One such tenet of this principle is that whatever harvest you desire to reap then you must sow that same kind of seed. If a farmer plants peach seeds he will grow peaches. If he plants apple seeds he will grow apples. If you love one another, you will be loved. If you help those who are in need, you will be helped during your dry season. If you extend friendship to others, you will find friendship in your hour of loneliness.

Whatever you want in life – money, love, friendship, etc. – you must first give that thing to the body of humanity and then God will return that which you have given, back to you a hundredfold. For example, if you want to love more you must first give more love to others. If you want to improve your finances and increase your wealth, you must first give of your financial resources to help others and to fund the agenda of the Kingdom of God.

The If/Then Clause

During my engineering career I have been involved with many new and emerging technologies. Most technologies require some type of programming subset that provides the instructions for the hardware to follow in order to achieve some task and quantity of work. One of the most essential commands in most programming languages is the "If/Then" command.

The If/Then command states that if a particular statement or situation is true then the system is instructed to take specific actions. As a matter of fact we use if/then commands to guide our lives and help define who we are. For example, as a child growing up in housing projects, we were taught that if someone hits you, then you hit them back. If a young lady warmly smiles at you, then she's interested in you and open to you initiating a conversation (assuming you're interested in her). And so the scenarios go.

This principle of sowing and reaping is based upon the same premises. You have to invest before you can get a return. You have to construct a dream before a dream can be realized. You have to give before you get.

But in sowing and reaping in life, there are three essential components of this principle that must be properly understood. The three components that must be understood are taking action, quantity of the sowing, and the benefit of leverage.

Taking Action

To actuate the principle of sowing and reaping, understand that nothing happens until you take the first step. To create a reaction you must commit to an action. The most important step in taking a journey is the first step. Successful people are successful because they have learned to take action and action defines who are they are and how they live their lives.

Quantity

To a large degree we can dictate the rate of return on the action steps that we take. There is a direct correlation to the amount that you sow and the amount that you reap. If a farmer plants more corn then he can expect to harvest more corn. If he is not aggressive in his planting then he should not expect much corn for reaping. Plainly put, the more you sow the more you will reap. The less you sow the less you will reap.

Leverage

When you sow expect to reap more than that which was sown. One acorn seed will produce a mighty oak tree, which will bear hundreds of acorns. One peach seed will produce a peach tree, which will produce thousands of other peach seeds during its life span. So it is with those of us who sow seeds to help others and to make our world a better place to live. Through the principle of leverage, God will take our attempts to plant seeds, apply His awesome and wonderful power to our feeble efforts and produce marvelous and spectacular trees of prosperity, well being, and contentment.

Tips for Implementing This Ssese Principle in Your Life

1. Nothing happens until something happens. Creating and building wealth requires that we invest before we have any chance of seeing a return. What do you have to invest? You have your time, your talent, your treasure, and your temple (the body).

2. Investing, or sowing, requires that we take a risk. Every farmer understands that when he plants his seeds in the Spring, there is no guarantee that every seed will take root and grow. Some seeds will most certainly never break through the ground and see the

bright sunshine. The farmer, however, steps forward and plants anyway, understanding the risk but believing in the potential.

3. Risk becomes more manageable when we increase the frequency in which we engage in the wealth building process. The more educated we become about how the process works, the greater the potential that we will enjoy the pay off from our investments. Therefore we must become players in the wealth building game. It is a good idea to start small, invest with others, and seek out good, sound, financial advice.

4. Diversity of seed planting is essential. Your investment dollars should be spread out among different investment vehicles. These vehicles include your residence, investment properties, mutual funds, stocks, bonds, entrepreneurial endeavors, and even your hobbies (i.e. art, stamp collections, coin collections, etc.).

5. If you are living right and living within the will of God, expect Him to move on your behalf and bless your seed planting. Expect God to do great things for you, take Him at His word and watch how He will reap your crops for you!

A Prayer for the Wealthy Minded

Dear Jehovah Shalom ("I AM" + Peace):

There is no one greater than You. How excellent is thy name in all of the earth and throughout the universe. Your Holy Word has taught us the importance of sowing first and then reaping the fruits of our labor. Not only did you tell us but you led by example when you offered up your Son, Jesus the Christ, so that your Kingdom might reap the many souls who would have been lost, had it not been for the sacrifice that was made by your Son at the Cross. Teach us that in every aspect of our lives we must plant good seeds if we expect a bountiful harvest. In the matter of finance, remind us that we must be willing to take some risks, diversify them, and expect You to activate your mighty power on our behalf. Help us to be patient but disciplined and wise as a serpent, as we seek to invest the resources you've put under our management.

Amen

Principle # 8: The Principle of Blessing Expectation

"And yet the same revolutionary belief for which our forebears fought are still at issue around the globe – the belief that the rights of man come not from the generosity of the state but from the hand of God…with a good conscience our only sure reward, with history the final judge of our deeds, let us go forth to lead the land, asking His blessing and His help, but knowing that here on earth God's work must truly be our own."
-- John F. Kennedy's Inaugural Address, 1961

A group of frogs were traveling through the woods, and two of them fell into a deep well that had cold, slippery walls. When the other frogs realized what had happened, they quickly rushed to the top entrance of the well to see what they could do. After assessing their running mate's dire situation, they concluded the well was too deep and the walls too slippery for them to have any chance of helping their friends out of the well and back into a safe environment. In essence they told the frogs that there was no hope and they were as good as dead.

Initially the two frogs ignored the comments and tried to jump up out of the pit with all of their might. The other frogs kept yelling at them to stop all their fuss because there was no hope and they were doomed to die. Finally, one of the frogs took heed to what the other frogs were saying and gave up. His limp body soon collapsed and slowly sank into the black, uncertain depths of the well.

In the meantime the other frog continued to jump as hard as he could. Once again, the crowd of frogs had concluded that his situation was hopeless and that he should stop his vain attempt to escape the confines of the well. But the frog jumped even harder and finally made it out. When he got out, the other frogs said, "Did you not hear us?"

The frog explained to his peers that he was deaf. In his mind he thought the entire time that they were encouraging him to make it and to survive. With their encouragement, he soon got to a point where he expected to survive and hop his way out of his situation.

Like these two frogs, many of us have found our way into deep, cold, and dark wells of financial difficulty and uncertainty. Much of our financial calamity has been self induced, and it seems like the world (i.e. friends, family, associates, etc.) takes special pleasure in our pain and suffering and symbolically begins screaming and yelling at us, implying that our situation is hopeless and that we can't/won't win.

While the words of the crowd affected the one frog in such a way that he expected his situation to grow worse and thus resigned all of his capabilities to receive and accept that inevitable outcome, the other frog thought differently. Since the other frog was deaf and didn't know any better, he took the same motions and visual cues that his partner had observed but he used his thought process and his expectation of what friends should do in a situation such as this to mentally create a scenario where he would survive and be saved.

Our God has not only the words to speak us out of financial miscues and mistakes but He also has the power to bless us with all the resources we need to create and manage wealth. However before we can benefit from this enormous power and resource pool, we must first train ourselves to expect God to do these things. God is able to do exceedingly, abundantly more than we can ask or think. But like in business, we must condition ourselves to expect great things from God.

Much of the management theory that is taught in today's graduate schools of business administration teaches that whatever you expect from people in your organization or team is exactly what you will ultimately get from them. If you expect them to be smart, creative and intelligent, they will end up being smart, creative, and intelligent. Conversely if you expect them to be thieves, dull, lazy, and stupid, then they will become just that.

This same theory is true in our relationship with God. So many people expect little from God and so consequently, they receive little from God. Successful people have conditioned themselves through prayer, meditation and life's experiences, to expect great blessings from God. They understand that they did not earn these blessings nor do they deserve such blessings. However, they receive the love, mercy, and forgiveness of God and usher in His many wonderful blessings. But what are blessings? Blessings are not necessarily the accumulation of material things. History provides thousands of examples of people who had every material thing known to humanity but who still lived miserable, dreadful, and unproductive lives. Blessings, properly defined, are the enjoyment of God's special and sacred favor. When God blesses us with something there is no sorrow associated with it. We are to leverage the power of God in our lives and expect great and wonderful blessings from Him because He is able and He loves us so very much.

Tips for Implementing This Ssese Principle in Your Life

1. Before we can expect God to do great things in our lives we have to first have big lives. In other words, God can't move on our behalf unless we have something that we are trying to do that is so powerful and big that God can work with it. One thing about God is that He loves to show off. God can't show off unless you give Him something big to show off with! He will take His children's dreams, use His mighty power, turn that dream into a reality, then sit back and watch the world marvel at His Greatness. Therefore, if you live an apartment and you desire to own your own home, go for it. If you are driving a 15-

year-old car and you'd like a new one, go for it. If you dream of increasing your net worth one hundred times more than what it is now and to cease living from paycheck to paycheck, then go for it. If God has placed in your heart the desire to take what are now uninhabited islands in Lake Victoria, East Africa, and turn them into a world-renowned conference center, a spiritual retreat, center and an international zone of peace, go for it!

2. Dreaming for dreaming sake is of no value. When we dream we must believe that we have the power to make that dream a reality. However, we must be careful. Believing that we have the power to achieve a dream is not just a function of our own finite power but more importantly, it is a function of God's infinite power. The strategic alliance or joint venture between us and God has no boundaries and there is no limit to where our dreams can take us.

3. God is no fool and He is the ultimate financier and entrepreneur. Although God can work through divine intervention to make things happen fast, he usually works through His human instruments and that means that we are to prepare plans to support our dreams. This is why it is so important for us to seek out God fearing financial advisors, attorneys, and accountants, to help us plan for our success. God may not have given you all the skills to complete the plan but He has positioned those resources within His Kingdom for you to access when you are of the right spirit.

4. Take your dream and your plan to the throne room of God, lay it at His feet and leave it there until He makes a move. Imagine that God is the Chairman of the Board of your company and you are presenting this new idea for your business that you are trying to get His approval of and commitment to provide the resources to make it happen. This is exactly what we do when we take our dreams and strategic plan to the throne room of God and engage Him in the process. Approach Him boldly with confidence and expect God to be convinced by your presentation and to activate the government of heaven to assist you, according to His will and plan for your life.

5. Recognize that God, as any Chairman of the Board, has the power to make any decision that he chooses that is in the best interest of the company (i.e. His Kingdom and your life). God may respond to your request in ways that will surprise you or in some cases, even disappoint you. Remember His plan and His will takes precedent over our own. He loves us and will take care of us but His will, will be done on earth as it is in heaven. Therefore we must trust God with all of our heart, mind, and soul. He may answer "no" to our plan but give us a better plan. He might say "yes" to our plan but suggest a few minor adjustments. He might say "wait until later," like he told me to wait ten years before my business really started to take off. He might flat out say "no" and direct you onto a completely different life track than what you are on now. You might be an engineer but he wants you to become a teacher for inner city children. We

don't know how God will respond, but we know enough to trust and obey His commands.

A Prayer for the Wealthy Minded

Dear Jehovah Tsidkenu ("I AM" + Righteousness):

I realize you are indeed my provider and protector. Forgive me when I have allowed the government of Satan to cloud my thoughts and to kill my desire and ability to dream. Renew in me a new and clean spirit and restore my mind and thoughts so I once again think like You, act like You, speak like You, and yes, dream like You, knowing that all things are possible through Christ. Teach me to expect great things from You so my life will reflect your power and might and that your name will be glorified and lifted up throughout the entire earth and indeed the universe.

Amen

Principle # 9: The Principle of Wealth Through Your Talents

"I give away riches and honor; wealth and prosperity are mine."
-- Proverbs 8:18

"But don't forget it is the Lord your God who gives you energy and ability to get wealth and to be successful. He does this because He loves you and because of the covenant He made with your fathers." -- Deuteronomy 8:18

"If you can do well and do good, you've won the game of life." These words, as spoken by Catherine B. Reynolds, founder of the Catherine B. Reynolds Foundation, exemplify a woman who has mastered the art of creating wealth through her talents. This foundation, which is poised to drop more than $500 million into cultural institutions in the Washington, D.C. area, exists because of the wealth that Ms. Reynolds has amassed over the last 20 years.

Hers is a story told many times over about ordinary people with extraordinary talents and an unquenchable desire for success and accomplishment. The granddaughter of immigrants, Catherine worked hard, leveraged her talents, became rich, redistributed it and ended up rubbing elbows with the President of the United States and other powerful people. The impact of this story is that this situation could happen to anyone who truly understands the power of their God- given talents.

But as I have had the opportunity to conduct workshops on wealth creation and entrepreneurship all over the world, I am amazed at how few people know or understand what their gift or talent is! Most people wander through life aimlessly, with no clue or inclination on identifying and using their talent for the glory of God.

If you're one of those people, don't worry and don't panic, just get going. There are usually some telltale signs that you can look for that will provide you some guidance on how to identify your core talents. For example, do a self-assessment to reveal those things that you really take pleasure in doing. What are those things that you would do even if no one was paying you to do them? What tasks do you really look forward to doing and excite you so much that sometimes it makes it difficult for you to sleep at night? Your answer to these questions will provide you a roadmap leading to your talent identity.

Another way for you to identify your core talents is to pay attention to which aspects of your life people constantly and consistently give you compliments. Is it your speaking ability where you are able to convince people to buy your product or even motivate individuals to take action in controlling their lives? Are you great at organizing events and bringing people together? Do you have outstanding instinctual gifts where you are able to discern critical events, even in what may be deemed chaotic environments?

The beauty of how God has distributed His gifts to us is that He (as usual) has been overly generous and provided us with multiple gifts from which to choose. By giving us more than one gift, He has increased the likelihood of us bumping into at least one of His gifts between the time we're born and the time we die.

God gives all of His children gifts and talents that if properly understood and used become the engines that drive us to achieve certain levels of success and wealth attainment. For Michael Jordan it was his physical talent that provided the engine for his business success. The tragedy is that most people don't have any idea what their gifts and talents are. It is a sin not to know and a tragedy if we go through life and never make the effort to find out.

While the list of possible gifts that God has given to humanity could be infinite, my research of the last 20 years shows that there are ten talent buckets into which the majority of identified talents can be placed. These talent buckets are:

• Factual Talent – Ability to remember and recall facts.

• Analytical Talent – Ability to analyze and come up with solutions to complex problems.

• Linguistic Talent – Ability to master multiple languages and dialects.

• Spatial Talent – Ability to recognize patterns and provide meaning to them.

• Musical Talent – Ability to produce and/or deliver musical products that are in high demand.

• Practical Talent – Ability to see the obvious when it is covered up by the unobvious.

• Physical Talent – Ability to compete in athletic events at a very competitive level.

• Intuitive Talent – Ability to predict the future and prescribed outcomes, given current and existing data.

• Interpersonal Talent – Ability to get along with and be admired by a diverse body of people.

• Spiritual Talent – Ability to maintain open and efficient communications with God and act as a conduit between God and humanity.

These talents that God gives us allow us to be creative. They provide us fresh and novel ideas that serve to solve the pressing problems facing humanity today. Our talents also allow us to improve our personal and corporate productivity, putting us in a position where we are able to do more with less and do it consistently. You see, my friends, God does not tolerate laziness and laziness is our refusal or unwillingness to find and use our talents to the glory of God. God warns us that a lazy man will soon be poor, but hard work will bring rewards to those who are diligent. A lazy person never gets what he wants, but a hard-working man gets what he goes after.

The bottom line is take action on actuating your God-given talent to build wealth and to benefit the Kingdom. Don't worry about the slack because God has got your back!

Tips for Implementing This Ssese Principle in Your Life

1. Opportunities to create wealth always are pulled by some sort of "vehicle." These vehicles include your job, your business, or your investments.

2. Let your talent(s) become the engine that drives your efforts to create/manage wealth.

3. Leverage the talents of others to drive your wealth creation engine. You leverage the talents of others when you:

a. Recognize you can't achieve true wealth without working with and through people.

b. Become confident enough in yourself that you are comfortable embracing the talents of others without feeling threatened.

c. Learn to share the wealth with others.

4. Focus your talents on making life better for humanity and the revenue and profit streams will follow.

5. Spend your life identifying and perfecting your God-given talent (gift).

6. Use your talent to increase your potential revenue streams while you work to decrease your living expenses. Only when your revenues exceed your expenses on a sustainable basis are you in a position to create wealth.

A Prayer for the Wealthy Minded

Dear Jehovah Rohi ("I AM" + Shepherd):

Thank you for providing me with so many wonderful talents and gifts. Please dispatch your mighty angels to mentor me on how to recognize and use them in such a way that I not only am able to create enough wealth to sustain my every need but, more importantly, that these new found wealth assets will serve to strengthen and expand your spiritual Kingdom. May my return on my investment in heaven, be great.

Amen

Principle # 10: The Principle of Contentment

"But godliness with contentment is great gain."
-- 1 Timothy 6:6

"And the soldiers likewise demanded of him, saying, And what shall we do? And he said unto them, Do violence to no man, neither accuse any falsely; and be content with your wages."
-- Luke 3:14

"Not that I speak in respect of want: for I have learned, in whatsoever state I am, therewith to be content."
-- Philippians 4:11

"Let your conversation be without covetousness; and be content with such things as ye have: for he hath said, I will never leave thee, nor forsake thee. -- Hebrews 13:5

The average American is bombarded with hundreds and maybe thousands of images and messages per day that define for her what money, success, and wealth means. These images include a Mansion, big SUV in the driveway, private school for your children, country club memberships, and spring break at Club Med.

The fact is that the average American has a lot to be thankful for because America, despite its numerous challenges, is the arguably the riches nation in the history of humanity. Consider for a moment the fact that there are nearly 5 million households in America with a net worth of at least $1 million. Our country is so wealthy that we spend more on trash bags than 90 other countries spend on everything!

Despite all of our material wealth, something is still very wrong with us. Consider that between 1970 and 1999, the average American family received a 16% raise (adjusted for inflation), while the percentage of people who described themselves as "very happy" was reduced from 36% to 29%. The sad truth is that we are more intelligent, better educated, highly fed, and spend loads of time and money to improve every aspect of our physical being. Yet our families are disintegrating, drug and alcohol addiction is rampant, the teen suicide rate has tripled, and social dysfunction has reached epidemic levels. We're consuming more but enjoying it less.

With this financial backdrop, it is easy to understand why most people struggle with the principle of contentment because the engine that drives our economy and is the underpinning of our culture is the desire for more. The story goes that John D. Rockefeller was being interviewed by a journalist and was asked the question; "Mr. Rockefeller, over your lifetime you have accumulated significant amounts of wealth, but I am curious, sir, how much is enough? Mr. Rockefeller paused for a moment and thought and then uttered, "Enough wealth is a little more than what I currently have!"

According to Mr. Rockefeller's definition, none of us would ever be content. But I beg to differ with Mr. Rockefeller because I believe contentment is a state of mind that a person creates for himself where he knows and has learned to be happy wherever he is in life. Contentment, properly understood could be perceived as "righteous discontent" or "enlightened striving." What these two terms suggest is that God is comfortable with us working to better and improve ourselves. The problem He has is when we put the accomplishment of these "things" before Him and when we freely compromise Godly principles and values in order to secure the "stuff" of life.

This principle does not mean we no longer strive for excellence in what we do. Contentment should never be confused with laziness, lack of drive or vision, or lack of purpose or professional goals. It suggests that contentment is found in the process of attaining the specific and specified level of success while maintaining happiness and fulfillment throughout the journey. Nor does it mean that we don't set high financial and business goals for ourselves and work very hard to achieve them. Most importantly, contentment does not mean that we necessarily approach the achievement of our goals with a lack of vigor, passion, and intensity.

Contentment does mean that if God decides that He will not add to our existing inventory of wealth in this life, then we would be just as happy and in harmony with His will as if he had blessed us more. As the old folks use to say when I was a child, "I am content in Jesus."

Tips for Implementing This Ssese Principle in Your Life

1. There will always be people that have more money than we have. There will always be those who live in a finer house, drive a more expensive car, vacation at more exotic places in the world, send their children to more expensive colleges, and who enjoy the best service that money can buy. If the Lord plants such desires in your heart to achieve, then go for it. However, if it turns out that these things are not in His will for you, then keep striving until you reach the level that He has destined for you on this earth. Remember that when it's all over, the first shall be last and the last shall be first!

2. As we are reminded in God's Word, seek out that position in life such that you are wealthy enough that you don't have to steal just to make it and embarrass God but that you are not so wealthy that you forget that it was God who gave you the power to earn that wealth and allow pride and misguided ambition to corrupt your spiritual self and miss out on eternity.

A Prayer for the Wealthy Minded

Dear Jehovah Shammah ("I AM" +There):

Thank you for the joy and happiness that you bring into my life each and every day. I recognize that there are no such things as "small" blessings or "large" blessings but that all blessings flow from thee and we are to be grateful no matter our position in life.

I pray Father that you would provide me and my family enough that we don't have to beg for our daily bread but not so much that we become haughty and forget about you. Position me at that point between poverty and prosperity so that I am perfectly positioned to serve out your mission for my life. It is at that point where I will find true contentment and my soul will be satisfied.

Amen

Principles of Wealth Creation in Position for God's Glory

Most people were asleep and the streets were quiet and deserted as Nicodemus made his way to the Mount of Olives, where the Master was dwelling for the night. Nicodemus, who was highly educated and held a high position of power in the Jewish nation, often advised the Council of the Sanhedrin to deal cautiously with Jesus. Somehow he sensed that there was something special and divine about this controversial man.

During the early days of Jesus' ministry Nicodemus had paid attention to the Galilean carpenter and was intrigued by the marvelous works He had performed. However, Nicodemus knew that he must take care that he didn't outwardly show admiration and respect for the ministry of Christ or he would face the hostility, wrath, and hatred of the determined but misguided priests and rulers of the nation of Israel. So, to satisfy the hunger in his soul and to prick his intellectual curiosity, he sought out Jesus under the cover of darkness.

In the presence of Christ, Nicodemus immediately felt Jesus' divinity flash through this human flesh. Jesus focused His holy eyes upon this man who, in Christ's infinite wisdom, was someone who really was seeking the truth and who, despite his position in the nation, possessed a surprising amount of wisdom. Christ used Nicodemus' good intentions and wisdom and got directly to the point that He needed to make with this Jewish ruler. With all the authority of His Father and limitless power of heaven, Christ sternly, yet kindly said to Nicodemus, "Verily, verily, I say unto thee, Except a man be born from above, he cannot see the Kingdom of God." (John 3:3)

Later, when Christ was crucified, rose, and ascended into heaven, Nicodemus remembered that secret conversation up on that lonely mountain and decided to come forward and reveal his belief that Jesus was in fact the true Messiah. Nicodemus quickly put his money where his mouth was and aggressively used his wealth, prestige, and considerable power to encourage the disciples and to fund the deployment of the gospel throughout the known world.

Although by the standards of the world, Nicodemus lost much of what he had owned because he committed it to funding the spreading of the gospel, he remained firm in his conviction that the most important investment we can make in this life is the investment in God's Kingdom on earth and in the heavenly Kingdom in eternity.

Like Nicodemus, Dr. Samuel DeShay and other committed people of God have committed their lives and resources to fulfilling God's eternal agenda. As I have sat at the feet of my mentors, men like Dr. DeShay, I have painfully learned that I am only a steward (manager) of my time, talents, treasure, and temple and that all my life energy must be invested in preparing the way for the return of our Lord and Savior, Jesus Christ.

As we stood on the hillside of Bugala Island in the verdant Ssese Islands, Dr. DeShay surveyed the expanse of the great lake and its natural beauty and in an almost hypnotic voice said to me, "Wallace, Christ will be returning to this earth very soon, and I can't think of a better place to greet Him than on these lovely islands." I humbly nodded in agreement and replied, "Yes, Dr. DeShay, that is true. But I pray that all of us will be ready."

This little book, The Ssese Principles, is a meager attempt to encourage you to be ready for this cosmic event. Jesus Christ's second coming is arguably the most important event in all of human history. By using the principles that are found in the Holy Bible and highlighted in this book, it is my prayer that the men and women of God will be successful at creating and building wealth in such a way that this wealth will be used to accelerate the return of Jesus Christ.

While applying these principles and committing ourselves to them will certainly help pave the way for Christ's advent, it will also make our lives on earth that much more focused and productive. Moses reminded us of such when he admonished the children of Israel, in his last "sermon," in the Book of Deuteronomy chapters 27 and 28; "If you obey the Lord your God and keep His laws that I have given you these last few days the Lord will bless you and make you greater than any other nation on earth." According to Moses, who spoke on the authority of the Word of God, below are the blessings that God will shower you with:

• God will bless you in the city and in the country.

• The Lord will bless you with healthy children and many descendants, and your herds and flocks will overflow with calves and lambs.

• The Lord will bless your vineyards and fields, and your baskets, kneading bowls and store rooms will be full.

• The Lord will bless you in your travels.

• The Lord will protect you from your enemies.

• If they attack you from one direction, He will scatter them and they will run in many directions.

• The Lord will bless your work and fill your barns.

• He will bless you in everything you do.

• He will bless the land of Israel.

• The Lord will bless you and make Israel into a holy nation as He Promised He would, if you keep His commandments and walk in His ways.

• The nations of the earth will notice how blessed you are.

• They will acknowledge that you are God's own people and will be afraid to do anything to harm you.

• The Lord will bless your land with prosperity.

• You will have large families, much livestock and rich harvests just as He promised.

• The Lord will open the windows of heaven for you and send you just the right amount of rain to sprout your seeds and ripen your harvest.

• He will bless the work of your hands so that you will be able to lend to many nations without having to borrow from them.

• The Lord will bless you so that you will become the leading nation in the world, if you pay attention to what He has said and faithfully keep the commandments and laws that He has given you.

• The Lord will bless you if you don't turn to the right or the left or worship gods of your own making.

About The Author (www.RobertWallace.com)

Robert L. Wallace is an accomplished entrepreneur, author, business consultant and internationally known speaker. He is the founder of three companies. The first company, BiTHGROUP Technologies, Inc. (www.bithgroup.com) is a successful information technology services company that specializes in wireless engineering, wireless network security, network engineering, software development, and information technology outsourcing services. He later founded EntreTeach Learning Systems, LLC (www.entreteach.com) which provides e-learning training services for entrepreneurs, intrapreneurs and micro enterprises. His third company, Techcom, LLC, is a technology commercialization company.

Robert earned his Bachelor of Science degree in Mechanical Engineering and Applied Mechanics from the University of Pennsylvania, his Masters of Business Administration from the Amos Tuck School of Business at Dartmouth College, and was awarded a Doctorate of Humane Letters from Sojourner Douglas College. Wallace has worked for such corporations as IBM, DuPont, Procter & Gamble, and ECS Technologies. He was appointed by Governor Robert L. Ehrlich, Jr. to be Chairman of the State of Maryland's Information Technology Board (ITB). Governor Ehrlich later appointed Robert as a Commissioner on the State's Advanced Technology Commission and the Minority Business Reform Commission. Mr. Wallace serves on numerous boards in the private sector as well. Some of these boards include the BaltimoreWorkforce Investment Board, the GE Center for Financial Learning, Maryland Hawk Corporation, the Gilman School, and the CENTERSTAGE Playhouse.

He has authored numerous articles and books on entrepreneurship, wealth creation strategies, intrapreneurship, and urban economic development. His books include "Black Wealth Through Black Entrepreneurship" (Duncan & Duncan, 1993), "Black Wealth: Your Road to Small Business Success" (John Wiley & Sons, 2000), "Soul Food: 52 Principles of Entrepreneurial Success" (Perseus Books, 2000), and "Strategic Partnerships: An Entrepreneur's Guide To Joint Ventures And Alliances" (Dearborn 2004). He is married to Carolyn W. Green and lives with his wife and children in Howard County, Maryland.

Printed in the United States
77292LV00006B/118-141